Michael Thomas was born and raised in the Ozark Mountains of North-Central Arkansas. He teaches composition and literature at Arkansas State University-Mountain Home. Poetry has sustained him as his true love and art since a child. He currently lives in Salem, Arkansas, with his wife, Kellie, and daughter, Sarah. His hobbies include reading, listening to music, hiking in the beautiful Ozark National Forest, and spending time with his children and six grandchildren.

This book is dedicated to all the poets, songwriters, and philosophers, living and dead, who have influenced, inspired, angered, and soothed me in a lifetime of reading, listening, studying, and writing.

Michael Thomas

ATHEISTS AND EMPTY SPACES

AUSTIN MACAULEY PUBLISHERS™

LONDON • CAMBRIDGE • NEW YORK • SHARJAH

Ordering Information
Quantity sales: Special discounts are available on quantity purchases by corporations, associations, and others. For details, contact the publisher at the address below.

Publisher's Cataloging-in-Publication data
Thomas, Michael
Atheists and Empty Spaces

ISBN 9781649797490 (Paperback)
ISBN 9781649797506 (ePub e-book)

Library of Congress Control Number: 2022911281

www.austinmacauley.com/us

First Published 2022
Austin Macauley Publishers LLC
40 Wall Street, 33rd Floor, Suite 3302
New York, NY 10005
USA

mail-usa@austinmacauley.com
+1 (646) 5125767

I would like to thank my wife, Kellie, for reading and critiquing my poems as I write them and when they are still in the roughest draft form, and for my two buddies at work, Alathea and Deborah, who read and comment on my poems even when they do not much like the themes presented.

Table of Contents

The Promises That I Keep
(A Foreword)

What author is there who, when looking at a text containing various portions of her or his life's works, considers the words written therein to be the vision she or he intended to reveal to fellow humans? I ask, is there such a person? Authors often pretend to know the meaning of their works and will quite as often defend what they have written either as youthful naiveté, religious superstition, or personal myth-making. They tend to think that they have presented what they believe as fact or what they perceive as an authentic idea that can be understood as *truth* to other people with similar intellectual capabilities and socio-mythical views. However, authors must realize that meaning will be conceded to readers, and, as their own readers, they are the first to notice a failure to convey even the most basic of concepts. They know, as all wise people know, that the interpretation of a work is not misled by dumb luck or an errant stroke of fate but that these interpretations are distorted by the author's immutable decisions. The most problematic of these binding decisions lies in word choice because it is in the selection of a word that most authors' revelations fail.

Words, their usages, and their arrangements are peculiar memes that have nothing in common with the natural relationship, cultural understanding, or social interaction that they are meant to represent, and a dictionary definition of a word hardly gives context for a reliable connection. Any author knew the word when she wrote it, but the word warped because she chose a word. Words organized into phrases and clauses exaggerate the vulnerability of word choice even further. Each word confined within a phrase or clause is naked before chilly gusts of misinterpretation but finds no protection surrounded by others of its kind. Conversations about or written analyses of an author's work as an attempted confirmation of an unbiased vision or a balanced revelation of the author's vision push the reality of her life and the honesty of her imagination into the fabricated and chaotic realms of nonsense. What author, no matter how hard she has tried, can present an untouched reflection of the world and her interactions and relationships with the things in it? After all is said and done, the essence of art is only smoke, color, and warp of memory, perception, and vision (past, present, and future) presented in vapid, ever-morphing words, words that can never be trusted to explain anything to anyone.

All art fails to satisfy the deepest desires of humanity because it cannot answer the two basic questions of human existence: "What does my life mean?" and "What happens when I die?" Those who seek the answers to these two questions in art are making the same regretful decisions that the artist who attempts to answer them makes simply because no reflection can answer these questions. Art does not answer such questions of ultimate truth. It only exposes superficially tiny truths and seldom even does that well. In the same manner, art does not give wisdom though it may expose folly, art does not dole out pleasure, but it may feed discomfort, and art cannot deliver happiness though it may inspire a profound sadness. While it may never grant its purveyors ecstatic joy, art can be a symptom but never the cause of bottomless grief. Art is sober, and it is violent, but it is always reflection and never the original experience.

A reader says, "This poet's work has caused in me insightful, sincere change" but had it not been this work, it would have been another, for this reader was looking for a likeness that suited an inner desire for change. Now, *change* is the mantra for poetry. "Make it new!" cried Ezra Pound in the 1920s, stealing the phrase directly from the ancient Chinese texts he was studying. Therefore, poetry must change or try to change and fail. It must change what it is about or not about, how it is formed or remains formless, what words it must use or not use, and who can or cannot read it, or it must fail. Poetry must become philosophical change, it must become social change, it must become cultural change, it must become political change, and it must become identity change, or it must fail. Poetry did become the elitist and intellectual property of the university and the doctoral critic, and it did fail. It did become the enigmatic typewriters of a million monkeys pounding out their versions of *King Lear* in formulaically incestuous poetry workshops, and it did fail. Poetry did become the diaries of eight year olds on Twitter and Instagram, giving what I have been assured is immeasurable pleasure to the masses of poetry lovers everywhere, and it continues to fail. Poetry, through all of this change or failure to change, has become enlightened and enlightening. More people are writing it, more people are reading it, and more poetry books are being sold than ever before in the history of the art. Hooray for Poetry and its changes! Hooray for Poetry's failure to change!

In all of this outside-of-the-box revolution, I see no flicker of incandescence guiding me through this dim-witted conversion or through the darkness of poetry's failure to transform. I, the simple maker of songs who uses words that you know and live with but do not know how to say, see no illumination.

I see no enlightened change for me because I never needed to change. I am always and only here to express that which is often thought. I cannot shift to a new thought but only repeat a thought that has been thought a million times before and millions of times afterward. You know this thought. It imagines your life, not mine. I only use the words of the thought because, maybe, I know the words. Maybe, I know the words better than most people. Maybe, I know the long history of the words and the thoughts and the people, and the words and the thoughts are part of the people that I know. I know how to arrange and rearrange the words to be about your thoughts. What I think is never about me, so I do not need to change. I can stay the same while you change, and I reflect your changes back to you in words and rhythms that you know. I am a simple maker of the songs that you know and live with but have forgotten how to sing.

I am always and only here to express your song in a way so that you say, "Yes, that is what I thought." This saying tells me that you are enlightened, but I cannot be enlightened by my own words. I can read Homer, Sappho,

Spenser, Shakespeare, Milton, Pope, Byron, Tennyson, Yeats, Frost, Eliot, Stevens, and Bishop and say, "Yes, that is what I thought." It is not a new expression but a thought that has been expressed a million times and will be expressed a million more times. It dreams my life, not theirs. I am inspired by their expressions, but I do not live their lives. I do not write their words but words very like theirs. I cannot see that words unlike theirs make anything new. I write inspired, or I do not write well. I do not write *new*. I am a simple maker of the songs that they knew and lived and continue to sing.

I do not have any answers to the two big questions, so I do not try to answer them, and even where I carefully or accidentally instigate change, it is painfully obvious that I am a fellow seeker who wrestles, like Jacob, with vague truths that I cannot hold, truths that both curse and bless me. My reflections, no matter how original in their distortions, are irrelevant if they do not articulate the same thoughts as my fellow seekers and if they do not use the same expressions as my predecessors. "Make it new!" is old and tired and wrong. It is the wrong words. It is the wrong songs. It is the exasperated expression of failure.

However, this wrongness is the same thought and the same expression that is found in all the symbolic portrayals of human failure. This failure is an old condition. This failure is a noble condition. The very essence of Greek tragedy is centered upon human failure whether the struggle against this failure is noble or not—and Shakespeare, the thought of Western thought, still has the market garnered on human failure. His gigantic portrayals of human failure cannot be superseded. However, we, the most recent of modern Western artists, have taken the portrayal of failure one step past Shakespeare's nightmares. We are no longer content in giving our characters calamitous faults. We no longer relegate human failure to the mishap of sightless reflection and wretched fiction. We bring our failure from within ourselves and are doomed to poetic abortion before we can begin our exhibition because of the fatal idea that we can successfully present ourselves as *new* characters in *new* situations represented in *new* modes of expression. We want to be the original and authentic characters of our inept plays and the clueless subjects of our hopeless poems, but we cannot be because every single player and poet represents a stock character that is not a genuine individual. We do not create anything *new* at all. We merely mock and then slander someone else's creation that is us. "Make it new!" Pshaw! We would need something besides words and thoughts to explicate ourselves from this tragic and utter failure.

The appropriate course of action following such a broad and startling claim seems to be to brace this hypothesis with various and sundry literary examples. Nothing could be further from the truth. Indeed, the study of the literary arts by over-eager theorists with no real sense of art is the main reason for the contemporary dabbler's inability to be a real poet. This failure was not really possible before the 19th Century and the systematic studying of literature because literature's disciples at that time were all readers. When literature's disciples apply themselves to an artist's work, they are reading. They criticize and analyze a work based on the aesthetic and intellectual values found within the work itself. They do not need to see or hear what Professor

Blotto has written or said about the work or what he says about the life of the artist. Disciples do not care to know which *ism* the work fits as if *isms* are as useful an organizational tool as alphabetizing or chronicling. When we, as post-critics, use these disciples' written applications to approach an artist's work and to attempt a final decision on the poet's meaning or a poem's value, we are not reading; the sacred and fundamental bond between the literary artist and her/his audience is broken. We become drone-like thinkers in cults of personalities, and every poem, short story, novel, and play becomes a school of thought, and no individual thought is left to be experienced as an isolated, imaginative, and co-creative event. With every critic and every school of thought, the value of an artist's work comes to an end for the studying-but-not-reading reader, and as Emerson said, "They pin me (the artist/reader/disciple) down."

We can only have a Shakespeare, Milton, Pope, or Blake in a world without literature students and without schools of literary criticism. Art—and especially poetry—needs pious, isolated, and individual converts, not congregations of prying critics. Poetry needs silent and solitary creative disciples, not schools of wisdom-seeking students. As readers, we must let the artist lead us, as Virgil led Dante, to the places we all must go, but we cannot so much as offer a single course or bearing upon the path, and we cannot go in large and clumsy groups. Sheer numbers cannot protect us from the evils and entanglements of a thorny literary work, but they can and do distract us and encumber us with the weight of their collective dullness. Poets are just as guilty of the herd mentality as any literary scholar and, in this, we all fail. In mentioning certain literary names to bolster my hypothesis, I have suggested a particular and well-worn path, and thus, I have failed. Please feel free to return to the paragraph that begins "However, this wrongness is the same thought and the same expression that is found in all the symbolic portrayals of human failure." I hope that you do not find yourself in a continuous circuit. Once you understand that art is about the failure to provide anything but reflection, inspiration, or creation, you may proceed.

The piles and piles of wood pulp and electronic bytes praising the works of the modern-to-contemporary author have never raised his/her effort to the level of poetry or art. When we place the modern-to-contemporary author upon a pedestal, how is it that we do not know that the likeness will sink into the fermenting mulch and digital abyss and rust, rot, or be lost on the infinite server? Most modern writers have already drowned in the flood of ink used to comment upon their sandy works. They are studied and interpreted, but they are not read. Only a few modern artists remain afloat in the stormy Sea of Ink, their highlighter-riddled, anthology-laden vessels in danger of being swamped at any moment. Most contemporary poets are praised, praised, praised on blogs, Instagram, Twitter, and other social media sites designed to present their divine inspirations in the context of secret insecurities and personal tragedies, which are made social and public for unacquainted, potential neophytes. Worshipped like technological Tennysons, they spend more time proclaiming the profundity of their idylls than actually giving them any depth of thought or clarity of rhythm. They will not drown in these shallow Seas of

Praise, but they will be trapped, like Heraclitus, beneath the mounds of manure spread over them and die of suffocation without being studied or interpreted because they smell so bad. None are new; none are original. The one difference between them and the poets and artists in the past, present, and future is that they will have never been read. They may be studied, they may be interpreted, and they may be worshipped, but they will never be read. In this, they have already failed, but, trust me, it is truly no great tragedy.

Since my words are doomed to fail and never present the vision, revelation, and reflection that I intended, why do I continue to write? Since I cannot advise anyone well about big truths or tiny, superficial truths, why do I continue to write? Since poetry seems destined, perhaps even doomed, to change and fail, and I cannot find anything in the past, present, or future that supports this change or failure even with myself, why do I continue to write? Since I cannot escape the times and could only ever be studied and interpreted by critics, post-critic readers, or worshippers or not read at all, why do I even bother to write?

I do have the answer to these questions. I write because I can keep a promise that I once made, and although I have long since forgotten to whom I made the promise, I promised that I would always write words in a poetic form that maintains a connection to song and the rhythms of my breathing. I promised that I would remain a priest to the fickle divinity of poetry to whom devotion earns little but trouble and lost time (Baudelaire). It is what I do, so I will write. I will write poetry. Promise kept.

Introduction[1]

Out in the Wild with Pen in Hand,
I thought beneath a Dogwood Tree
When suddenly a naked Man[2]
Appeared and sought some Words with me.

"Write a Verse about all Men
And I will tell you what is wrong."
And scarcely had it left my Pen
When He cried out, "These Lines are much too long."

So, I scratched out a Line or two
To show Him that I made good Sport.
"My God," He sighed, "What's wrong with you?
This Poem is too short."

"Start over with the Words, 'He was,'
And end it with the Words, 'He died,'
And in the Middle say, 'Because
He dreamed, He was not satisfied.'"

Then, I turned His Verse to Heart
And hid my Pen beneath a Stone.
I told Him that We too must part,
And then I left the Words alone.[3]

Atheists and Empty Spaces

We have no more hallowed places,
Empty spaces, or penitent faces.
The bees who buzz in winding races
In petal, pistil, style, and stem
Have no fond memories of him.

All we know is the diurnal traces
Through which the sun silently crawls,
Low, swollen, drowsy, and faceless,
Stretching and stretching cold shadows
Along our endless ignorant races.
In that glow, all dreamy and dim,
Live no fond memories of him.

Flowing through the empty spaces,
Flinging off its many faces
Like autumn leaves in windswept places,
Anima[4] imagines endless mazes
And chases ever-changing sexes
Through the many mythic phases
Of the ancient goddesses' whim.
She's no fond memories of him.

Now, fallen idols fill the faith
Of noiseless, tasteless, empty space
While acid tears flow down the face
Of graces lost in Christian arts.
Theatrics and aesthetics, no!
Anesthetics[5] sooth and smooth hearts.
Graceless and nameless marble parts
Deny the loss of face and limb.
They've no fond memories of him.

When Time comes to change our places,
When Days desire empty spaces,
And the shadows turn to bony faces,
June bugs chasing bobbing daisies
Will declare the human race is crazy
To mock the insect's mazy flight.
Sanity lies in soulless limbs
And no fond memories of him.

We know no more hallowed places
Except in those empty spaces
Where careless creatures buzz and crawl
Into the smiles of atheist faces
With petals, pistils, styles, and stems
And no fond memories of him.

Wedded with My Memory

I choose to unite with safe Memory,
The only one who yields at my request
And raises walls against my enemy,
Time the Stalker, who will never rest.
I cling to her as Months and Years sneak by
Searching for the hidden home where I lie
Afraid of the pain Time may force on me
When he crashes in an unwelcome guest.[6]

Time, himself, will creep over my body
And leave his mark upon a fragile thing.
My nimble limbs will grow weak and knotty,
My vision, a blur, and my ears will ring
At every whistle above a whisper.
With Memory, my actions stay crisper,
And even when dear Hindsight is spotty,
I hear very well how the birds did sing.

When I sleep, she comes to me in dreams
And brings a thousand faces from my Past.
All admire what I was, and so it seems,
I cannot be forgotten in the vast

Margins of cumulative Memory.
Time, here, is stumped by inconsistency,
For we can bend the instants to extremes
And cause fleeting seconds to last and last.

If I choose, she can put me in the womb,
Though this is not a conscious resolution,
Or stand defiantly over my tomb
And witness against my life's conclusion.
We can kiss again the first girl I loved
In a retouched time that will not be moved.
For all these things, Memory creates room
In the span of a speck's revolution.

Therefore, 'tis Memory I'll take to bed,
And though I'll have no children with this wife,
My progeny will live inside my head,
And all who see my sense will think I'm rife,
With good intents for those unborn children.
Besides, who knows what will or might have been
Had I not wedded my Memory instead
Of the reality of Time in Life?

The Buzz Revisited Again[7]

These rapt simple silences speak
Of the random order that *was*
And not of the omens we seek
In the forbidden name, *The Buzz*.

All is accidental when *All* is art,
Else is predictably wicked or worse,
A dream without a definitive heart,
A mark on the forehead meaning a curse.[8]

Cursing still, the lamp is shattered,
And light dissolves in whirling Dust.
Creation is the thought that mattered
And *All* the buzz that ever *was*.

The rousing rain and wildly willing sun
Seduce moist blooms and brashly bulging stems
To breed and seed with conscious senses stunned.
Am I condemned to grow such thoughtless limbs?

One among millions, mindless bliss,
One among millions, vine and creep,
One among millions breezes kiss,
One among millions craving sleep.

Yet sleep is not consistent with *The Buzz*,
Even if I barely do remember.
It is a waking dream, a sentient fuzz,
Mocking lips burned with an ancient ember.[9]

Consulting Self, I'm sure to find
A balanced passion in the breast
A potent impulse urging Mind
To matters it can mimic best.[10]

I sing the fan electric that nightly sings to me[11]
For its harmony protects the fidgeting of my brain,
For its noise hears what I do not want to
And filters it,
For it causes me to sleep even when I have no dreams.
Oh! Hardened steel skeleton!
Oh! Durable plastic fan arms!
Oh! Three-speed magnetized motor!
My mind is enveloped in your indifference
And you pause me in the midst of livid schemes!

No more mocking! *All* is lost!
The Art is mine! But at what cost?

Now that I have a craft to sell,
You may well ask, "What is It?"
Scuttling backward into my shell,
We will pay *The Buzz* a visit,[12]
While all the buyers come and go
Speaking of Parmigianino[13].

And there is no time to revise,
Nor time for taking of the tea.
Going inside may not be wise
Because this *Buzz* was meant for me.

Know thyself, then[14]; all thought is calm,
All deep silence is holiness,
All prayer feeds a desolate palm
When praising gods of emptiness.

The Buzz is frenzied, overjoyed,
Singing, crying, laughing, reaching
Out of the convalescent void
Into the mad prophet's teaching.

Mad prophets? Now, there is a buzz!
A sense sublime speaking through
Some inner voice like conscience does.
What else have the good gods to do?

Tomorrow, *All* will have been done,
And we will have no need to fear
The flippant hymns of feral fun
New poets hate, but long to hear—

Nor will we rhyme,
Nor have consistent meter,

Nor temporal rhythm,
Nor sense Outside the Mind.

Part 1: The Burial of the Head

(Abusus non tollit usum)[15]

New words learn arrogance, sleeping
Like babes under woolen blankets,
Sweating and smelling of violets.
Powder dries the moisture of sweet
And rapid growth, and poets fuel
The hectic need to understand
Through nipples of paper and ink
Like our Mother's own tongue-worn breasts.

We wring the milk seeping with dreams
Like spring rain down thatched eaves.
One drop, one word, caught in the web
Of a bright prism of rainbow
Almost never reaches the ground,
Almost fails to sprinkle the Dust,
Because we tied it to our thoughts.

Welcome to the big empty world!
Drip upon drip upon daisy!
Eat fruit to make the dream milk sweet.
Eat Crow to create bitter cream.

Form, form the same shapes from the Dust
To make the words of What It Was.

Non sum qualis eram,[16] I think.
I am not what I used to be.
Muddy ditches, swollen rivers,
Empty boxes filled with letters,
Barren wombs ignoring pleasure
Of humming, buzzing, breeding ease.

I lay on my right side three days[17]
As a sign of foes approaching.
Three years and I will build siege-works.
These words are dreams to wet the Dust.

I lay on my left side three days.
Three years and the great walls shall fall.
These words will freely feed the Dust.
I was naked for seven days,
Seven years to stumble as slaves
And on day three of the eighth year,
The poets will be pure again.
The Dust will be given vision.

But, what does it reckon for me?

I saw flowers with three petals,
One for each stage of crafting life:
Innocence, Practice, and Patience.

I eat them slowly for a time.
Each is sweet and filled with Bees.
Yes! Bees buzzing hither and back.
The workers and pubescent queens
Sleeping in sheets of swollen dreams,
Eating nectar and creamy pollen,
Bursting and thrusting at the seams
Like shy and secret succubi,[18]
Giving Samson his fierce riddle,[19]
Tearing down the pagan temples.

The taste becomes stiff like metal,
Like a tent stake through a forehead,[20]
Like slaves' blood in godless water,
Like a bronze viper on a cross, [21]
Or silver tainted by a dance.[22]

Oh, no! Oh, I fear I must stop!
I have tasted too much of Death!
The petals are words of Ashes and Dust!

Until I eat the bud of Easter time,
Then, lilies bark bright and yellow,
"One will suffer, but all shall live."
Yellow and black, buzzing, alive.

I gave the wind three directions.
One blows high in rocky dreams.
There, words drip in luminous streams.
One breathes deep in the heart of sea.
There, salty words seal wounded souls.

One is life for Ashes and Dust.
All words are of a will. *Eli! Eli!*[23]

God spoke his Word, and the wind died,
Where all spirit is shaped in ice,
Where words are born and crystallize.
As if there might be something there
That God does not want me to hear.
Forgive me for my mind of ice,
For my frozen watery words,
My petrified praise and doubt.
I think I always knew
The Unknown God was the Poet.[24]

And when He sings of Eastertime,
Life springs full-grown from the image,
And all the angels rock and roll.

Part 2: Mating

Do not brush this goddess aside.
Her affections may be contrived,
But she will make a suitable bride.
With stumps for legs, how can I hope?
With nubs for arms, how do I dare?
There is no intercourse with her,
But business does not need a whole.
Thirty pieces of silver, no?[25]

I do believe that she[26] has lips
That moisten with rousing pleasure
And a comely suggestive voice
That moans within her insane parts.
She's marble lungs that draw no breath
Across a hungry marble tongue,
She's perfect round and weightless breasts
Where drops of nectar could be hung.
She's a flat, hairless, marble V
And from behind, a luscious urn
Sprouting an elegantly snaking spine
To a neck that causes heads to turn.

Her hair is rich and lushly thick,
Like a sponge for sopping my sins.
Wet and waving, how would she drape
It across my hard pink body?[27]

Woman, lift yourself! Fly above me!
Spread your flowing, flying tendrils
Over the length of pulsing flesh!
Am I cold? Am I dead, dead cold?
Do not say I am stiff and limp,
Or we would have a paradox[28]
And I might love the missing parts
Rather than the extant whole.
This is still a financial deal.

Change her eyes; the eyes must be changed.
Tell her, Father, replace the eyes.
In that soulless depth of pure white,

I can see where the water flows
Miles and miles to the edge of the earth.
She is not thinking about me.
She's falling into empty space.
Her ship with seven swollen sails
Goes over the edge, not plunging,
But gliding into some vain sea,[29]
And, plainly, she does not love me!

"Ah! But, Son, we have a contract."

Someday—we will gauge normal life
For "when"—the arms and feet will grow,
And I will trade a tit for tat[30]
And all parts will presume the whole.
My words of love will long for limbs,
And paper will melt marbled ice.
Someday, the sting of poetry
Will swell the inspired fertility
And I will ride her round the world.

She does *not* love me! Yet I think,
The Dust is rising at her feet.

Part 3: The Sermon of the Hound[31]

(We are the dogs that feed on the crumbs.)

Blessed be the trickle of the stream o'er rocks
And the many lusty scents 'round the pool.

Blessed be the running sheets of morning fog
In the breezes above the squirming trees.
Blessed be the silent one holding his bay
At the senseless chatter of clownish squirrels.
Blessed be the hunt.

The hound does not come before the Master,
Yet he sends me ahead to see what's there.
When I say, "Come! It's here!" sometimes he does,
But he often whistles me back to him.
He knows that I would chase the faintest scent
To hell 'cause I keep my nose to the ground.

I do not worry for my meals.
I hunt, and the master feeds me.
If I do not hunt, the master feeds me.

I carry his commands close to my heart:

1. Come.
2. Stay.
3. Go.
4. No.
5. Sit.
6. Hush.
7. Get in.
8. Get out.
9. Fetch.
10. Give.

But greater than all commands is "Listen."
The master's gentle hand upon my head
Is better than a cool drink of water.
The master's pleased voice in my happy ears
Is better than a warm, lumpy gravy.
The safe and playful shouts of his children
Are better than a meaty shoulder bone.
To run and hear his firm footsteps follow
Is better than a day of sunny sleep.

The coyotes sing of masters long gone.
My master is the glory of my song
And shall not be forgotten while I breathe.

I sing:
Blessed be the one who does his master's will.
Blessed be the hunt.
Blessed be the essence of our worthy prey.
Blessed be the running buzz of quick spirits,
The wind in my face, the sun on my back.
Blessed be the master first and, then, his hound.

Part 4: If by Water

Thomas the near-sighted doubter[32]
Walked on the face of the water
And peered into its murky depths.

Oooo oooo ouch!
The piercing prick of the splinter

From that frazzled and timeless yoke,
The dense burden of creation
And the weight of separation
Hurts me deep within the linter[33]
And the fuzz of my first ginning.

Land from Sea and Light from Chaos
Are the angst of unborn masses
Of atheists and pessimists,
Poets, all, who feel the movement
In the deep and dang'rous waters,
But still crown the misfit swimmer,
Unseen Leviathan[34], their king.

King of the Dead and King of Frogs,
Birthed in the brine and water-logged,
He never sees the sky nor sod
And worships wind as the one god.
He cannot envision an heir,
Nor harken to a subject's prayer.
He rolls in sea-borne sand, and must
Have never known the life of Dust.

Second Thomas[35], the devotee,
Devised a pious poetry
And walked upon the barren grave
Of all the water sprites and nymphs.

I can only mention these three,
Thomas, Second Thomas, and Leviathan.
The Water returns to the Sea,

And the Word finds a buoyant soul.
This Soul has a skeleton made
From Dust, which shall be recompensed.

Part 5: From the End, Beginning

Who is the lone geometer [36]
Measuring an ample circle
And tracing tawdry line on line
Who does not find a centered self
Of the balanced whole he has made?

He sighs, he moans, he cries and pouts,
But finds his own stirring of stone
In the ring where he lives and dies.

With downy wings of Dust and spit,
He once explored the loft of will
But found no water on the hill,[37]
Only the "dead mountain" hiding
The curse of the forgotten dead,
Walking on the waterless mountain.

Dejected, he formed more circles
That spiraled down and down and down
Into the prime anatomy
Until he ran out of rhythm.

BUZZ!

The sun and stars presume to move,
Propelled by the torment of Love,
And, with no love, he lies inert
In a dirty little belly.
BUZZ!

A black-haired woman fiddles. Yes!
And tinkling marble strings tighten,
So that the wind, a northern wind,
Sings across the finely tuned threads.
These harp strings, plucked one at a time,
Like petals from a daisy, hum.

And somehow he listens to them.
Humming, buzzing, he hears their song;
For three days, he learns to mock their chords.

Rock and no rock, the oath of stone,
Is rocked and rolled away from him
And breath is given to this Dust
From The Movement On The Waters.[38]

Creation is *All* that mattered
And *All The Buzz* that ever was.

No Arbiter Needed

We cannot see things eye-to-eye
When you relegate your sphere
To a supernatural being
Whose motives are not clear,

When tragedy might be a test
Or a system to adjoint[39]
A symbol from ancient fairytales
To prove a struggling point,

When it works in mysterious ways
And its thoughts are not like ours,[40]
When it treats both good and bad alike
With its omitted powers.

No, we cannot communicate
Unless we make one thing clear.
I bargain with you and you with me;
No gods need interfere.

If you care to offer a prayer,
Let it be we both may keep

Our business based in what we know
Not ghosts that haunt our sleep.

I know a thing unknowable
A form never reflected,
Whose designs are indiscriminate
And always unexpected,

Whose randomness fits bad or good
On the whims they all may toss,
And that is why neither you nor I
Need rulings from Chaos.[41]

Carnalville[42]

The city trades cravings like poker chips
With conceit at the center of its schemes.
It mimics a ribald apocalypse
Concealing symbols of lust in its themes.
Contortionists twist on disjointed hips
While naked children of dragons breathe fire.
I lick a crust of fried cake from your lips,
Whetting your thirst for my nib[43] of desire.

Coins tinkle and clink out of crystal plates,
Dull darts ricochet off half-filled balloons,
Memory tiles turn without any mates,
Fortunes are forfeit to deceitful runes[44].
The fates all seem fixed, the odds so askance
That few go away as lovers of chance.
Very few ever leave lovers of chance.

My eyes are tempted by two ample breasts
On a woman too petite for their size,
"Push the right button," she sweetly suggests,
"And lovely lady will get big surprise."
"Try it," you say with an excited squeal,

Unaware how I am being seduced.
She touches my arm as she primes the wheel,
And a pleasurable pull is produced.

"Use your fingers," she purrs into my ear,
"It is important to play pleasing game.
The rewards to come may not come right here,
But lovely lady will like all the same."
In steady circles, my fingers caress
The smooth button as I study her eyes.
When I see them widen, I firmly press,
And you and I slip away with a prize.

New lovers grope madly on a wild ride
That marks their time like a blazing comet,
And they stumble away half satisfied
Smelling slightly of pin grease and vomit.
Calliope music prods them along
Though nobody knows the name of the song.
No one ever needs the name of the song.

A strapping young carny in a Ratt[45] shirt
Admires your form from his cover of smoke.
You are aware that he's trying to flirt
And seem to want what his actions provoke.
I stake my claim with a kiss to your neck,
And you accept with a self-assured sound.
He leers as we leave the ride's wobbly deck
Wrapped in the rhythm of Ratt's "Round and Round[46]."

Some lovers lose faith in this illusion,
Trust fractured in a kaleidoscope light.
They wipe their love in puerile[47] confusion
On the sullied blank sheets of the night.
You and I slip away from this stark mess
To a certainty our sense understands,
To unite in the chaotic darkness
With experienced and diligent hands.

Carnalville dissolves before the sun glows,
So too its shifty lights, games, and faces.
It only lasts as a livid dream goes.
In the pure light of day, it erases.
Why was it here? Nearly anyone knows.
It mimics hell and fills empty spaces,
We dream of hell to feed empty spaces[48].

The Knowledge of Stone

The fresh grass and raw flowers
Wave wildly in a breeze
Like the Love that is ours
To tend, scatter, and tease,
Before we give what we do own
To the knowledge of Stone.

Stone seems perfect enough,
Mounted in its proper place,
A sound symbol of Love
In nuptial embrace.
And gambol about, Stone will not,
Nor will it ever rot.

Not much like Love is Stone,
For it is very still
And keeps as well alone
As weeping idols will,
So let fresh grass and raw flowers wave
Over the gelded grave[49].

A 21st-Century Song

(How Poetry Is Donne)[50]

Find and fetch a flailing line,
Hang a maker[51] worth a hoot,
Skip upon a chapbook's[52] spine,
And tell me if you feel a foot.
Train pendulums to alter time,
And nonrecurring words to rhyme
       And still
       Fulfill
The current poet's monthly spiel.

If you care to catch odd things,
Noises ingeniously born,
Listen as that poet sings
Like a murder of crow in the corn;
Then, if you can learn it, please repeat
The eerie lyrics, but be sweet.
       What ear
       Can hear
After scanning verse so queer?
If you meet a meter, move back
Though it tempts you with its beat;

Its sire is some silly hack
Who will sell his soul to eat.
The true poet, if she is pure,
Writes only with a pulse obscure
   And swears
   Her ears
Are naturally attuned to Jazz[53].

What Dreams May Come

(In honor of and inspired by various poems of John Keats[54])

The Prologue: Where John Keats Would Not Go

Porphyro and his Madeline[55] are gone.
These lovers fled away into the storm,
But reckless tales of passion linger on
And seldom does the fiction shift its form.
A hero seeks a lady soft and warm,
Asleep, she longs to be his loving wife,
Her dreams of him, like bees, come in a swarm
And drown in sweetness all their mortal strife.
Such sleeping beauties rarely come to life.

Still, as John tells us, on St. Agnes' Eve,
Young virgins might have visions of delight,
So is it any harder to believe
That drowsing men have fantasies at night?
They feed their dreams erotic scenes but light
Their egos with distortions of desire
So that they often willfully lose sight

That passions spent in visions don't require
More than arousing notions to inspire.
The muses in man's dreams are not divine,
Their *music, yearning like a god in pain,*
May just as likely be four cups of wine
As any saint or angel with its train.
To augur life in fantasy is vain.
This woman's face was in a crowd last year,
The reason for her presence is quite plain;
The mind remembered, and she did appear,
But how aroused and naked is not clear.

I'll talk of dreams like good Mercutio[56],
But I'll not have my hero leaving free.
He will be trapped in deeds he does not know
And hounded by the dogs of memory.
Bewildered by her sensuality,
My Porphyro can never be so bold
To break his Madeline's sweet reverie
And pull her from a dreamscape's carnal hold
And, thus, he'll always be out in the cold.

Part 1: Out in the Cold

On a scarred hilltop stripped of all its trees,
A man lies quaking in a wooden cage,
A crib that blocks nor warms the cutting breeze,
A monument to someone's icy rage.
He lies in slushy mud, nose to his knees,
And shivers as he searches memories

For who it was and what he has done wrong
And why that person's hatred is so strong.

A freezing drizzle falls from steely skies
And melts in puddles on the muddy floor.
It mixes with the tears that sting his eyes
Until his ducts deliver them no more.
He kneels against the rope-tied door and pries.
He thinks he must break out before he dies
And leaves this world not knowing what he's done
Or who would torture some poor mother's son.

His trembling hands test every stick and knot.
His mind recalls each adversary's face.
He pokes his limbs through every open slot
And finds the poles fixed firmly in their place.
No weakness can he find, not one damned spot,
Nor enemy whose ire would be so hot
As to condemn him to a death of ice
Without so much as seeking alibis.

The daylight fades into a falling snow.
He has no blanket nor a stitch of clothes.
Can he survive this night? He does not know.
The odds seem greater with each breath he blows.
Yet human noises haunt the woods below
And haloes rise above some man-made glow.
His hopes revive; he starts to walk in place
And thinks tomorrow he may plead his case.

Sometime near dawn, the snow clouds blow away,
And bitter northern winds shake ice-gripped grass.
The man's tired shuffle hardly is a sway;
His feet are freezing in the crib's morass.
When the black darkness cracks with a new day,
He deems his only option is to pray
That one pretending god will end his wrath;
And, look, a wraith appears upon a path!

The specter, moving slowly, wears a hood
And carries in its hands a pot or plate.
It often stops and stares back at the wood
As if its burden bids it hesitate.
The prisoner feels no qualms and if he could,
The indecision would do him no good,
For, in his mind, the phantom in the cape
Is now his first and best chance to escape.

Part 2: A Memory Materializes

As the caped figure nears the wooden jail,
The captive seeks a face beneath the pall
And finds a visage that he knows quite well,
But, with its age and anguish, not at all,
A lover from his youth, now pale and small,
Who once was tan and supple, fit, and tall.
He whispers her first name from memory
And hopes it is the key to set him free.

She does not seem to notice nor reply
But sticks a rock-hard biscuit[57] through the gate.
Through blue and trembling lips, he asks her, "Why?"
She quickly turns to leave as if she's late.
In desperation, he cries out, "Please wait!
I need some explanation for this fate.
Are you the one who placed me in this spot?
Whoever might have hurt you, I did not!"

She stops; he sees she's bare besides the cloak.
Her feet are raw and red against the snow.
She then acknowledges the words he spoke,
"You're here because of me. Now, I should go."
"I'm here because of you? How is that so?
I felt that you belonged to me, you know,
But then your indiscretions caused our end.
You are the one who slept with my best friend."

"That has been years. The bad feelings have died.
That deepest cut is seldom on my mind.
We cannot fix old heartbreaks if we tried,
So it seems best to leave what's past behind
And tolerance should be returned in kind,"
He claims and scans her shaded face to find
A spark of understanding or regret
Yet what he finds he will not soon forget.

Part 3: A Matter of Perspective

No amnesty in her heart can be won;
His pleas have no effect on her cold stare.
She really must believe that what he's done
Is crime enough to keep him captive there.
He'll freeze and die. She simply does not care
That her sense of the past seems so unfair.
But if she felt his life should soon conclude,
What motivated her to bring him food?

"Why did you bring me food? I need to know.
Apparently, you still want me to live,
But if you keep me caged here in the snow,
I doubt I'll be persuaded to forgive.
Perspectives of the past are relative,
But perceived threats can cause us to misgive
And lead us to a judgement rash and harsh
As penning a man in an icy marsh."

A notion came upon him as he spoke;
The melting snow and slush no more did run,
His goose-bumped skin has smoothed as if a cloak
Has warmed him and revived him like the sun,
Which, suddenly, throughout his cell has spun
A glittering web of warm rays, and one
Of those beams draws him to the woman's face
Which now reveals no hatred—not one trace.

Her guise has altered to a lusty glow,

His eyes fall to the curving of her breast,
He feels a stiffening tingle down below
And blushes at the way that he's not dressed.
She pulls her robe aside to bare the rest
Of a form Aphrodite must have blessed.
Then, all his thoughts of how compassion goes
Are overwhelmed by passion's pulsing throes.
He reaches through the bars and grabs her hips;
He pulls her back against the wooden cell
He probes a finger in her moistened lips
And gently rubs a hardening pink swell.
He pokes his penis through the gate, but Hell!
His shaft can't reach the wetness of her well.
Still, he can't stop what thrusting has begun;
Before they quite get started, he is done[58].

In spasms of release, all light goes dark,
And deep within he feels a sense of shame
As if he's been some sadist mistress' mark,
A helpless pawn in passion's wicked game.
But now, he knows the woman's not to blame;
All his relations tend to end the same.
He gazes at the lady with no clothes
And sees in her shape every "she" he knows.

Part 4: The Persistence of Memory[59]

He falls exhausted to a still-damp ground;
The gloomy storm clouds gather overhead.

Nearby a dove is cooing, but the sound
Is like old Charon[60] calling for the dead.
"It seems that in this cycle I am bound
As any string into a ball is wound.
Please offer me, if it can be, advice
On how to end this awkward sex and ice."

He half expects that his one earnest plea
Will fall upon the coldest of deaf ears,
But as he struggles to a muddy knee
And braces for the advent of new tears,
She tosses him a golden barrel key
And says it is the charm to set him free.
"I hardly see, when caged in sticks and rope,
How this outdated bauble gives me hope."

"You are here in spite of me. I do not lie
Though I am but a figment in a dream.
You put yourself within this cage, not I.
Contrition is an intermittent theme.
You fashion forms like me as succubi
To hold you and expose you till you die.
Each time, you are seduced and semen spilt,
Then, lack of consummation becomes guilt.

What you've left incomplete, I do not know.
I only voice the words you have me say.
This former girlfriend's shape, this cell, this snow,
Are mental reminiscence run astray.
In dreams, you let your past afflictions grow
So that they overthrow the status quo.

You've brought me here so I might set you free
And ease the persistence of memory.

The totem[61] synchronizes with a lock
Impeding progress of past fantasies.
Redirecting mindflow, you may block
The repetition of these reveries.
Yet, memories are not set like a clock;
They stream through time as water 'round a rock.
You might direct a brook to a new course,
But floods will overwhelm you with their force."

She says and pulls the cloak around her tight.
The wind has brought the pattering of sleet.
"Well, I think I'll survive another night,"
He flings the golden symbol at her feet,
"These concepts may be real but they're not right.
I have no guilty conscience, I need fight."
Saying thus, he curls up on the floor
And swears he will be dreaming her no more.

Epilogue: A Place Where John Keats Can Go[62]

No more, dear John, we'll live through dreams no more:
No nightingales, no fairy girls, no knights.
Ruth made a husband on the threshing floor
And not among incestuous Moabites,
So we should be inspired by plain sights
And not the foreign fancies of our dreams.

We'll seek our guidance in authentic lights
And not where shadows fill our minds with seems
And other more destructive psychic schemes.

The dreams of gods are real and smoothly pass
Into immortal blisses sweet and pure,
But in night's visions, warped like wavy glass,
No finite human spirit can endure.
We saw the shadow; now, we are secure
That it was merely nothing in the night.
We walked into the depths of the obscure
And neither held nor loved its dread delight.
Do we wake or sleep, John? I think we write![63]

Love, Light, and Song

Love melts me into glass for you,
A Tiffany[64], a Dalle de verre[65],
A grisaille[66] your rays imbue
With colors of inspired air.

In silver matte[67], I hold your light
And cast it into empty space
Filling the void of darkest night
With warm reflections of your face.

On your brilliance, I frame my song,
I feed your sunshine to my words
Who love the light and sing along
Like luminous, enchanted birds.

Thus, as the truth, my lines endure
To show your light and grow my art
And bound by love both bright and pure,
They lighten every darkened heart.

The Message[68]

I sent an agent.
"Do not come," the message read,
And still it came.

The sun rose and set.
The skies were red but turned blue,
And still it came.

I did not slumber.
The hairs on my chin turned white,
And still it came.

I did not whisper.
Rumors fled an empty house,
And still it came.

The herald that I sent
I assume no longer lives
Because it came.

It knew what I planned
When I warily requested,

"Do not come,"
And still it came.

On Chains[69]

Can poets find an inspired path
That is not bare with wear
Or meet an artist from the past
Who has not come from there?
What traceless space can still exist
Above a printed ground?
And, once below, what wanton hope,
Or unique dream, or novel thought
Has not been redundantly bound?
Yet the dogmatic critic still complains
When any poet locks his Art in chains,
For safety binds it to his heart with chains.

'Tis true, the Wind will never cease
Though airy words die out.
And while the Sun may always burn,
Quite clearly, so will Doubt.
Some Ignorance must be preserved
To ensure Faith is blind,
But new Religions must be built
For innovative Fools to find
That Freedom is aberrant to our Brains

And every sinner goes to Hell in chains
And every saint ascends to Bliss in chains.

Some people move about this world
Believing they are free[70],
As if cavorting without bounds
Grants immortality.
They think they encounter choices
That mute a rigid past
And affect a certain future
That cannot come too fast.
They think, they move, they laugh, they cry,
They believe they are all free, and then they die.
Each day, the sprightly ballerina trains
When every dancer's forced to dance in chains
And every poet writes these words on chains[71].

A Carpenter's Man[72]

I help build scaffolds[73] for scholars
On platforms no sage will see,
And, as long as they're framed in dollars,
My conscience will be free.

I form a faith for atheists,
Within Christian liberty,
And the founding father deists[74]
Say my conscience should be free.

I help craft crosses for racists,
Who honor their sanctity
By burning them in their bases
But their consciences are free.

I draw my sword for Jesus
Since my sisters and brothers agree
That the pagans are here to seize us[75],
And our consciences must be free.
Our consciences must be free.

Big Maggie McClain[76]

Just off the crest of Pilcher Ridge,
A half mile from the Steffen Bridge,
On a north slope covered in moss
And haunting moans where the winds toss
The deep silence of the valley,
No coward would ever dally
Near a stone house mortared in ivy,
Nor any person with half a brain
Hoped to cross Big Maggie McClain.

A lot was said but little known
About this waif who lived alone,
Who rarely strayed into the light
And must have done her chores by night—
But, really, who was there to see
Or witness what her habits be?
Who would offend her privacy?
No one! None dare invade her space.
Such misery hung about the place.

Know her? No! But everyone knew
Above her house the black crows flew

In riotous murders of cackling caws,
Callous and critical guffaws,
Until a gunshot shushed their cries
And shooed them off to kinder skies.
Was it she who drives or she who plies?
For always they would be right back.
Filling her air with hectic black.

And round her house a grove of trees
Twisted by malicious breeze
Grasped like hands sprung from their graves
Yet chained in dirt, as Earth-bound slaves,
Begging mercy from sinless skies
—Or this appeared to prying eyes
Who watched afar Big Maggie's
Offbeat and mysterious ways
With never more than an ignorant gaze.

But some do know, and I am one
Who's learned a bit of what she'd done
And how she came to be alone,
Since she won't know what I can tell,
I'll fear no vengeful witch's spell.

It's true Big Maggie's place was cursed.
For growing crops, it was the worst
Lying beneath a rugged northern slope
Where only moss and briars could cope.
All winter, it was in the shade.
All summer long, the shadows frayed
To hot slivers like shiny blades,

Clipping any green she might grow
And searing every seed she tried to sow.

But Maggie's place was in a line
Between the Wilson house and mine,
And every youth and all his pals
Were bewitched by the Wilson gals[77].
I, like Noman[78], was also drawn
To these young nymphs with cheeks like dawn
And eyes that sparkled in the sun,
Full lips that smiled a life of dreams,
And breasts that took men's breath in teams.

Needless to say, their siren's song
Was sung, and it pulled me along
Like any sailor with a torch
To crash upon the Wilson's porch.
Since more than time might have been lost
If I had been afraid to cross
Big Maggie's land right near her house,
I filled my heart and soul with grit
And tiptoed by right next to it.

A year or two, I drifted by
With both my feet ready to fly
If I saw the woman we all feared
Or a blackguard sentinel appeared.
None ever did. I met her twice
And both those times she acted nice
And offered me some tea with ice
Which I refused without one word

Because of all the lies I'd heard.

Big Maggie was not large at all.
In fact, her frame was rather small,
But she filled out her blouse and jeans
Like other beauties in their teens
Though her tanned brow wrinkled with care
And gray streaks tinted her black hair.
I sensed a whelming sorrow there
In her forced smile and bleary eyes,
And they caused me to realize

That this sad woman meant no harm
To any life upon this farm,
Not on the ground nor in the air
Nor any being anywhere,
But she had chosen this dark hole
Because it mirrored her own soul
Of which she could not gain control.
She let her deep torment and pride
Corrupt the outs and her inside.

I saw her twice and not again,
So it should seem the stories end.
I never spoke; she spoke to me
And I acted quite cowardly.
Though other people thought me brave,
I only signaled with a wave,
But now Maggie is in her grave,
I can tell the tales I know
'Cause Little Maggie[79] told me so.

In the attic, fastened up tight,
Were chests of photos, black and white,
Handwritten letters marked in red,
And lines of verse, one that said,
"Freedom is just another word
For nothing left to lose." I'd heard
Those lyrics somewhere. It occurred
To us both, and who could blame us?
Maggie's beau was someone famous[81].

We scanned the letters left and right,
Found "help me make it through the night[82],"
And "Make believe for the good times,"
And sundry and assorted rhymes,
Most of them spoke of love and hurt,
Beer for breakfast and for dessert,
Searching for a clean dirty shirt,
But for her surcease of sorrow[83],

It's hard to say what we did next,
But as we looked through all the text,
We found an open letter never sent,
And you may be surprised at how it went.

"Dear KK,
When we were broke in Baton Rouge
Waiting to hop on a train,
I was feeling about as worn out as your jeans.
That night, you thumbed a semi down

Just before it rained
And he drove us on in to New Orleans.
You took your mouth harp from your bandanna
And played it softly while I sang the blues.
The windshield wipers kept the time
And I held your hand in mine, and
We played every song that trucker knew.
Do you remember how we called those the good times?
We hitchhiked from Kentucky to the California coast
Sharing every secret of our souls.
Though all kinds of weather,
Through everything we did,
I did my best to keep you from getting cold.
Then, one day near Salinas, you quietly slipped away.
I was looking for a home
Because I had to find one.
My belly was getting bigger every single day,
And I felt a body growing inside of mine.
Now, she's two years old, walking and talking,
And we're both doing fine—
And I feel every tomorrow,
You will be coming back our way.
I know it's just a matter of time.
Love always, for the good times, Maggie McClain[84]."

***[85]

So that is the end of this story,
But, readers, please don't worry.
I know Maggie deserves a bigger tale.
It was simply too damn boring

73

And your author started snoring,
And the lies that he was telling
And the lyrics he was stealing
Made him feel like such a felon
That he'd rather cut this yarn
Than go to jail.

And what of that cursèd rhyme scheme?
Who was I trying to mimic?
I'd bet a dime Shelley or Keats[86].
It perturbs me like a bad dream
Or maybe like a psychic
Who records her portents for Yeats[87].
Oh, boy! "Mere anarchy is loosed upon[88]" this poem.

"Declaring the end from the beginning…" [89]

Just off the crest of Pilcher Ridge,
A half mile from the Steffen Bridge,
On a north slope covered in moss
And haunting moans where the winds toss
The deep silence of the valley,
No coward would ever dally
Near the stone house mortared in ivy,
Nor any person with half a brain
Hoped to cross Big Maggie McClain.

Cupid Warns Psyche About Her Sisters[90]

Here I am, now.
Close your eyes.
Put out your lamp.
Feel my zephyr breath.

I cannot be here.
I must go,
But do not soothe
Your sisters' woe.

Perfect love, oh, Psyche!
Cannot dwell
In the bitter light
Of Envy and Suspicion.

The Shadow Feeds

The melting day flowed over hills
In fountains of red-golds and pinks,
The spring buds glittered frosty green
As the dust on a fairy's wing,
The last light skipped across the lake
In twinkles of flickering winks,
The shadow's crawl
Swallowed it all,
An impassive, ravenous snake.

A Love Song, or I Am Your Whole World[91]

If my breath was the wind,
I would whisper and send
Your soul scattering through the air.

If my eyes were the sun,
I would blind everyone
To the unbending love we bear.

If my hands were the sky,
I would capture each cry
Escaping your lips when you're blue.

If my heart was the sea,
I would rise up and be
A wave that comes crashing on you.

If my lips were soft earth,
I would bury your mirth
In murmurs too fine to perceive.

I am your whole world
And your pure love is furled
'Round a life that my wishes weave.

Learning to Curse

Whoever guesses, thinks, or dreams he knows[92]
About the empty spaces all around
In reckless ropes of ignorance is bound.
A naïve noose does his bold neck enclose
As he ascends gallows of holy prose.
Is wisdom there or death? Has he not learned
That to the light the artless moth is turned,
And, in illumination, it is burned?

Madness makes humans dream that they are free
To pluck religions from wild words of faith,
To be inspired by a sacred wraith,
And pardoned from their worldly misery
By dying idols hanging in a tree.
If His image is hung there, let it rot.
It is but food for buzzards and is not
A proper symbol for unsullied thought.

The poet, too, presents persistent lies
Sharpened to snip the *nazir*[93] from his life.
He makes Delilah seem a loving wife
With all the new and unused tropes[94] he tries[95]

That gouge and rip what's hallowed from our eyes.[96]
Like that sly temptress, the author withdraws[97]
Once he's revealed the gravest of our flaws—
No temples can protect us or our gods.

We face a world full of wonder and awe
And, in our minds, imagine more sublime
Than what is captured in our space or time.
Yet, life[98] is best consumed when it is raw
Not half-digested in some artist's craw
Or misinterpreted from cryptic verse.
Of this false pair, we choose not which is worse,
But Nature knows that either is a curse.

Revelations[99]

He asked, "What did it say to you?"
While cunning lingua[100] flicked his ear.
Into his thoughts, her hot breath blew
Pleasures indulged not knowing fear.

He probed, "How did it feel to you?"
As eager hands pressed swollen fruits.
A pleasant numbness pierced him through
His soul into his stony roots.[101]

He moaned, "I dream that we will die"
While 'round his waist her legs entwined.
"I told you, Man, the Bringers[102] lie.
Let worldly knowledge ease your mind."

He sighed, "This is the joy of life,
To feel no fear of wrong nor right[103],
To know my mind, to know my wife."
With this, her clasp became too tight.

He cried, "I feel that this is wrong,"
And tried to twist from her embrace.
"That may be so, but before long,
This Eden will be empty space,

And you and your too trusting Eve
Will sow your seeds and birth your sons,
Whose daughters will freely conceive
The offspring of the Ancient Ones[104],

And we will fill this fledgling world
With pleasures suited to our state..."
And on and on lost Lilith[105] purled[106]
As Adam worried for his mate.

He begged, "What will you do with me?"
With heart and ribs both set to break.
"Oh silly man, you surely see
God made your kind to serve the snake."

The Day Rain Filled Empty Spaces

The clouds are fat.
The raindrops twinkle.
From brim of hat
To toe, they sprinkle.

The Earth transpires[107].
Dust becomes mud.
Ssshhh! Say the tires
In a paved river flood.

It's tap, tap on the roof,
Peck, peck at the windows,
Noiselessly aloof
Until a gust of wind blows.

A mist-filled twirling breeze
Refracts a farmhouse light.
It glisters[108] in the trees
And waltzes through the night.

The rain falls where it may
On just and unjust places[109]
But won't forget the day
It filled all empty spaces[110].

Shapeless[111]

We pass through idolatrous[112] places
Where deities cannot go.
We are becoming shapeless.
Our apathy makes us so.

We enter ourselves in races
No mortal has ever won.
Infinity is shapeless,
And we seem too bored to run[113].

We amble through empty spaces,
Indifference our wavering guide.
We are becoming shapeless
As we shift from side to side.

We think that in most cases
The truth is what we have seen.
Our faith is growing shapeless
As the glow around a screen.

I mark the passive faces[114]
Bound in cellphone screen ennui.
They are becoming shapeless,
Strangely alien to me.

I ask how they embrace this
Living through an avatar.
You say our lives are shapeless
And these memes[115] are who we are.

We are kings of infinite spaces,
You explain in a nutshell[116],
For the Internet is shapeless.
Oh, I know that story well.

While you sift through herbs of graces,
You may pick Ophelia's rue,
And as you grow more shapeless,
Hell itself will tire of you.[117]

Admiration[118]

Dread this daughter of ignorance[119]
And the toxic delusions[120] that she makes.
Her charming smile turns noxious grin
'Mid nests of hissing snakes[121].

Her transient form mocks Wonder's awe[122].
She is a terribly beautiful crone.
She stirs the hearts of admirers
But turns their minds to stone[123].

Her blood gives birth to wealth and art[124],
Her assent educes deep devotion,[125]
Though she dies a party favor[126]
Bereft of emotion[127].

Oh, Happy Days! They Dream but Not of You

I.

What happy days! The people play
As all unwitting do
And carry on their merry way
And dream, but not of You[128].
They think dear life is deep enough
To pack their sacks with empty stuff
And search for nothing new.
They place faith in words of sages
Whose dated thoughts fill cryptic pages[129].

II.

I will not ask them if gods age
Or if idols mature.
I will not ask them how they gauge
A timeless life so pure
That it endures beyond belief[130].
I will not raise god's image in relief
So clerics might immure[131]
A demi-man within a myth
And make a living god to bargain with.

III.

I dare not ask them if You change,
A trait all too human.
A mortal god is mighty strange[132]
And apt to illumine
A simple mind's imagination
About the facts of creation
Which I am assumin'
Was the making of all things only once
But that one time in fruitful abundance[133].

IV.

I dare not ask what they may know
About a faith that's real
When any time the wind does blow
They turn to it with zeal
And feel they are the first cocks to be blown.
The lucid world has always known
How windswept zealots feel
And marveled when the flocks gather
To blow back at the wicked weather[134].

V.

Oh, happy days! They look and see
But do not understand
That all their myths are poetry
Beyond their rude command[135].
Their sacred book is much too long
And brimming full with bits of song

Of a highly styled strand
Of which they only fathom bits
Without straining their feeble wits.

To Nature

I remember those moments when we loved,
When moon and stars, neap tides[136] and time,
My raw emotions moved.

I reinforced those motions in my mind
When dust and mud, blithe[137] dew and drop,
Two kindred wills[138] did bind.

Now, weeds scream green
And red buds cry,
Trees weep, creeks roar, rocks groan;
So I…so I,
No longer care
To mingle in the chaos there.

The science myth[139] has bent our bonds apart
So wind and rain, glass sand and sun
No longer warm my heart.

What principles[140] conceive I cannot touch
While snow and storm, hoar frost and flood,
Show me you feel too much.

Spring lilacs brown,
May lilies dry,
Roses crisp, and daisies burn;
And I...and I
Refuse your will
And seek more empty space to fill.

A Love Song

We had only kissed,
Or if we had,
What we had missed
Was not so bad.
Or do I mean it was
Good as absence goes?
All I know is
A need arose.

A rose as a kiss,
A remnant of some sun,
Is little more than this
Now that it's done.
It is a trite conceit
With mild blushing hues
And throbbing jealous feet
Tap-tapping lovesick blues.

The facts get hazy
On some sweeter parts;
Memory is crazy
About broken hearts

And driven madder
Still when it does find
The one time we had her
Was a slip of the mind.

"Had her" as in "kissed,"
A brushing of the lips,
But the lips missed,
And so the past slips
Into a moving mist
Of endless blisses
And being kissed
A thousand perfect kisses.

A Postmodern
Poet's Complaint[141]

You are the worst to cry the muse is gone
As any rhymer I have ever seen,
Yet this week you have tossed off nine

Pages of less than wretched verse.
None of it is Wordsworth-worthy, of course,
But in any monthly you'll find much worse.

While it's true you do owe much to copy,
Your imitations are seldom sloppy
And more like Byron than like Southey.

To listen to your moans is tough
When I have lost the muse myself,
And that is why you piss me off.

At least you know your beans from Burns,
A lesson I have never learned,
So that, when stumped, my mind is perned.
(Check out Yeats, you moron!)

Get thee behind me, you pedantic hack,
Blackguard, scoundrel, bibliophiliac!
You've got my muse; I want her back!

Stop your reading! Curse those damned books!
Burn your Shelley and all his stupid works!
Poets with learning are nothing but jerks!

Of Gods or Monsters[142]

Love was but is not
The wax on a feather
Before it gets hot.
Icarus[143], yes,
That is us.

Love knows that it raises
Around minotaurs
Inescapable mazes.
Daedalus[144], yes,
That is us.

Taught by the spider,
Love cuts not a thread
While it is inside her.
Theseus[145], yes,
That is us.

Jealousy is Love's death,
The searing, white sun,
The tomb for the bull god,
The Dionysian isle,

The spark of the gods
In the theistic myth.
Prometheus[146], yes,
That is us.

Emma Jean[147]

Just off the rolling, lusty hills,
Where nightly sing the whippoorwills,
On down the softly sloped incline
Whiskered with oak and erect pine,
Over the mossy sand stone crags
Where mist mellifluously drags
The dry creek like cotton candy
In a spinning machine
Lives a will-o'-wisp named Emma Jean.

Sightless since a sudden fever
Robbed her vision like a reaver,
She does her best to recreate
The memories of her sighted state,
But she forgets what most is true.
The fever took her mother too
And left no color for her art.
Her ample flair is flawed
With no fervor left in a broken heart.

Lost with that love, so too the guide
To paths of a more sensual side,

For Father's heart, much like her own,
Has hardened to a polished stone,
Pleasant, perhaps, to look upon
But cold and hard when light is gone.
Of normal desires, she knows not
Nor anyone to teach
How to take warm thoughts and render them hot.

So pink has disappeared and red
Was never in her naïve head.
Rosy urges, pure and tame,
Left with a yellow sense of shame.
Perhaps she should relate to blues,
The saddest of the many hues,
But she can never jot them down.
With all color lacking,
Her art is scentless, tasteless, senseless brown.

She does not paint with green or red.
Yellow and blue to her are dead
Recollections of what was sight
Before her world turned black and white
And all her upsides became down.
She only dabs her brush in brown,
The hue she does not want to be
Though it's the way she feels,
And fashions representationally.

In fact, she paints by sense of smell,
Occasionally, touch as well,
But lately, it seems, she has found,

She cannot paint by sense of sound.
She finds the echoes quite absurd
For silence is brown as a bird
And a midnight rain shushing down
On the cabin's tin roof
Bores so broadly it brushes itself brown.

People come from neighboring towns
To buy the blind girl's dabbled browns
Daubed on used blades from old saw mills
That trimmed the timber of these hills[148].
They pay as much as fifty bucks
To stare at scenes with abstract looks,
To wonder what it is she sees,
And guess what is not seen
In her monochromatic memories.

When patrons come to get the blade
Of rustic art for which they've paid,
They say of a saw painted brown,
"What a great bear or tree or fawn!"
And Emma Jean furtively smiles
And flexes her artistic wiles.
"It is whatever you want it to be,"
She confirms cunningly,
"I only pray that one day I will see."

Thus, pity keeps them coming back
To feign the love of art they lack.
Alone with Father and her fame,
Each day, each thought, passes the same,

None the better or none the worse,
Which is the core of any curse,
But neither of them think it odd,
That in this empty faith,
They blame the blindness on the will of God.

Maybe not "God," but some spirit
Causing pain so Man might fear it,
Yet who offers solace for a soul
Who wants her life out of control
—Or her restraint as it may be—
Ordained by some dark deity.
Atheists only learn to hate
The most contrived excuse,
"My life is not mine. It belongs to Fate."

Father supports this point of view
And clings to it as most men do
Whose children suffer random ill
That is not cured taking a pill.
Her art goes on denying griefs
And life goes on through blind beliefs,
But sometimes thoughts began to stir
As healthy needs arise,
And these urges do much to disturb her.

This summer morning after hay,
When busy work is put away,
When locusts drone and light has weight,
She thinks she'll paint a horse's gait,
Its neigh, its scent, its clippy-clop,

The ripple of its skin—but stop!
She hears the ring of steel on stone,
A horse trots up the creek
With a strange rider, and she fancies him alone.

She puts him in a leather hat
Pulled low over his face so that
His eyes are hidden from the sun.
His cowhand scarf, a wild rag one,
Is loosely tucked into his shirt.
His blue jeans bound with leather girt
Are neat but fraying at the seams,
His cowboy boots are worn.
He looks like a lover she's seen in dreams,

And this scene sets her to smiling.
Just to make him more beguiling,
She imagines a confidence
That is quite nearly arrogance
In the way he sits his saddle.
Then, she slyly adds a rattle[149]
Since she senses certain peril
In his sensual odor
That is bafflingly refined—and feral.

She smells a man not young nor old,
A voice that's warm, a heart that's cold,
Rough hands with strength but soft to touch,
White teeth that shine a bit too much,
A wiry frame concealing might,
A shadow not revealed by light,

And when she senses he is near,
Those feelings fly away
As his scented breath caresses her ear.

With southern drawl as smooth as silk
And buttery as fresh-squeezed milk,
"What is this thing?" he asks of her.
"Why, it is you on your horse, sir,"
She admits with a final stroke.
"Surely, you make a feeble joke,"
He laughs, "All that I see is brown."
All she can see is bits
Of light as she comes close to falling down.

With no training in female charms,
She fakes a faint into his arms,
And finds that he is not surprised
By coquetry so ill-disguised.
He lifts her smoothly to her feet.
She smells his skin, she feels his heat
His beard tugs her hair in tangles,
She perceives all his points
And ponders his many manly angles.

"I'm sorry I spoke out of turn,"
He says as her cheeks start to burn,
"But it has never crossed my mind
That any painter might be blind.
Still, if I may offer advice,
A little color might be nice,
And adding some pinks and purples

Might liven this dull art
And appeal to more dynamic circles."

"Your perspective is not like mine,
I believe I am doing fine.
I make money. I fulfil a need.
Purple, cerise, colors, indeed!
And what would colors do for me?
Do you think they will help them see?"
Her senses stun, her nostrils flare,
She is so excited—
But the anger gives her a potent scare

As colors flash through her dark mind,
The first she's seen since she's been blind.
"Colors, sir, are not what I feel."
She lies, feeling them a great deal,
"Besides, I know where all this leads.
First to desire, then other deeds
That bring a foolish woman down.
I will not be seduced…
By…" Then her fervor fades into a frown.

With her senses so keenly drawn,
She notices his aura gone
As if some breeze had blown him by
Or some dark spirit from the sky
Had pulled him back into the brown
And left her burning all alone.
Then, just as quick, his scent returns,
His hand touches her hand

And the warmth of skin like an acid burns.

"Try this," he says, and on her nose,
He dabs the petals of a rose,
And lightly slides around her face,
The perfumed leaves as if to trace
A form onto her passive soul.
A sob escapes; out of control,
Her darkened eyes begin to weep,
"Please, stop," she says, "I can't
Do this. My principles are lodged too deep."

But then a weight presses her lips
And something sweet and sticky slips
Between them and awakes her tongue
To yearnings for more fruit that's hung
Tantalizingly close at hand.
"This is much more than I can stand,"
She cries, "Please tell me what to do.
Forgive my artlessness,
But here I am[150]. What can I give to you?"

His hand clasps firmly on her wrist
"I'll only take what you insist
And give you what you need for now."
He murmurs as he smooths her brow
With warm and tender angel's lips.
She puts her hands upon his hips
And trembling wholly pulls him near,
"We must be quick," she moans,
"For my father will not approve, I fear."

Still in the languid afterglow,
The lights like golden honey flow
Around her naked arms and thighs
"I know that you must have green eyes,"
She utters as her fingers find
And feel his eyelids, "In my mind,
Their hue is like a walnut leaf
Or a light emerald
Or calm waters around a coral reef."

He nips her hand with a quick kiss.
"All will be color after this,"
He says and rises from her bed
"Your anger will be dark but red,
Your sadness may be tainted blue,
But every mood will have its hue,
And here is the important part,
Do not forget this thought,
I'm now and will forever be your Art."

Without a sound, a scent, or trace,
His presence fills then leaves the place
And Emma Jean is all alone
Quenched with color to the bone.
With hushed mind and body yearning
Back into her pleasure turning,
She sifts her fingers through her hair,
And suddenly wonders,
Was her sly stranger really ever there?

Through the evening hours, she gathers
Passions bright as peacock feathers.
An art she's never felt before
Flows like sunlight into her core
Filling the pink of virgin lips
With red perfumes of rosy hips
And guiding timid searching hands
Through violet desires
And sunset blushes of exotic lands.

Now twilight falls over the hills
And doves moan out their parting trills,
The orange moon floats in lilac skies
And Emma, feeling blue, just sighs.
A glow beneath her bedroom door
That has never been closed before
Tells her that Father waits outside
Confused, bemused, worried,
But not so willing to swallow his pride.

With cautious air but easy charm,
She sits by him and takes his arm,
"I've been asleep for hours it seems,
And had the most unusual dreams.
Perhaps next time you go to town,
You'll get some other paint than brown.
It's time for me to test the feel
Of diverse sensation
And recreate a thing that is more real[151]."

He only sees her hair astray,
A confidence, a curve, a sway,
An aura of experience
Where once was only innocence.
He notes two buttons and the eyes
Are open to the prying skies,
Revealing curves of swelling breasts,
That will tempt lustful eyes
And encourage many unwelcome guests.

He doubts that she's aroused her self,
But how…seduced by someone else?
She's just a girl—with no mother—
Can she know about a lover?
She will be used; my God, she's blind.
Such thoughts are all that fill his mind
"I hope to God he's gone away."
He puts hesitantly,
Uttering words he never thought he'd say.

"Father, dear Father, do not fear,
I am and always shall be here,
But there is a deep change in me,
A light I've felt that makes me see
How all my art is full of sin
By holding what I feel within
And keeping all sensation out,
Out of my art and me.
I've learned that wonder is what life's about.

Tonight, I will delight in dreams."
The silence hangs for hours it seems
As Father thinks what this may mean,
To him, to art, to Emma Jean
"But, you are …" he begins to say
As she gets up and glides away
Like a moonbeam across the floor
"Shhh," she says and pauses,
And closes his thoughts with her bedroom door.

Out her window, the glowing light
Fills empty spaces of the night
With spirits from the lands of dream.
On her brow, an heraldic beam
Sparks miracles inside her mind
And shows her why she has been blind
And how tomorrow she shall see
What passion does conceive
And how conception[152] sets the whole world free.

Just off the rolling, lusty hills,
Where nightly sing the whippoorwills,
On down the softly sloped incline
Whiskered with oak and erect pine,
Over the mossy sand stone crags
Where mist mellifluously drags
The dry creek like cotton candy
In a spinning machine
Lives a will-o'-wisp named Emma Jean.

No Access to My Pain[153]

It[154] has no access to my pain,
It cannot feel my trembling thoughts,
It is no ghost inside my brain,
So all I am to it is lost.

My stories are a troubled tale,
In which my friends are damned to hell,
And enemies all die as well
At the casting of ruthless lots.

I took with me a galley oar
And headed inland to a home
Till someone asked me, "What's that for?"
And now, I sit here all alone.

I have no walls, no guarded gates.
I have no will to keep it out,
And all my loves and all my hates
Have surely died before their times.

I pitch no prayers to empty space,
I pour no wine on godless ground,
And should I name it in this place,
    It has no access to my pain.

My Soul Is Dark

For GGB and LC[155]

I.

My soul is dark—all that I feel
Is in my ears or in my eyes
Not in some obsolete ideal
Of giant gods in empty skies.
If I, some hope, may yet maintain,
It must be in the aim of Man,
And in the power of the brain,
To master that which it can scan[156].

II.

Yet in the mind some sense is deep,
A voice, a hum that must be heard,
That rouses doubters from their sleep
To search for that unerring word,
A true word silenced far too long,
Or not a word, a perfect chord,
And not one note, but the whole song
Like David played to please his lord[157].

He Said There Is No God[158]

He was born to parents poor as dirt
And never knew a moment's peace.
His life was full of loss and hurt,
Cathead biscuits[159] and bacon grease.

His mama prayed, his daddy cursed.
Somehow, they made twelve kids.
Two died right after childbirth,
Most likely due to SIDS[160].

He was the fifth and in the way.
He was granted no room to grow.
So he stayed small and then one day,
He fell prey to polio[161].

The fever nearly did him in,
But the pain, Mama realized,
Was not the punishment for his sin[162].
For that, he was paralyzed.

With no spare time to take care of him
And no money for any meds,
Any help for the child was slim
In the small house full of kids

So he went to live with his Pa and Ma
Who made sure that he did eat.
For four years, he could only crawl,
Dragging his dead legs and feet.

Where he found strength, nobody knows,
But his arms grew big and strong.
When he felt a stinging in his toes,
He would walk before too long.

Sometime the same year his sister was raped
By a deacon from the church,
He pressed himself up off the steps
And stumbled across the porch.

Chorus:
I watched him live, and I watched him die,
And never, one time, heard him curse.
I witnessed many a deep felt sigh,
But hardly any worse.
Still, I turned away from his grave
With no teardrop in my eye
Until I heard a stranger say
As I was passing by,
"This man's sad lot in life is done
And they've covered him in sod,

But do not cry for this man, son,
For he said there is no God."

Now, walking well, he walked to class
And learned fairly well from his books.
Then, Mama took a cough in her chest,
And he had to go to work.

Thirteen years old and bucking logs,
Giving Daddy the money he made,
He lost a finger to Dixie skid dogs,
But never got repaid.

Each evening around the campfire,
The loggers shared their jug.
He hardly had a dark chest hair
Before he felt the tug.

The liquor didn't give him rest,
But it sort of led him to it.
He liked the very strongest best
And found out how to brew it.

His first still was a small turnip[163]
His second was a submarine,[164]
And with it he made more lettuce
Than he had ever seen.

He spent a summer at his set-up,
Cooking mash and hunting game,
And spent many a day in a cup

Till the Revenuers[165] came.

At his young age, they let him go
On his withering mama's vow
That he'd never breathe a still fire's smoke.
(He uses propane now.)

Mama, she died in a powerful pain
Crying violently to her lord,
Her service was just one more thing
Nobody could afford.

Chorus:
I watched him live, and I watched him die,
And never, one time, heard him curse.
I witnessed many a deep felt sigh,
But hardly any worse.
Still, I turned away from his grave
With no teardrop in my eye
Until I heard a stranger say
As I was passing by,
"This man's sad lot in life is done
And they've covered him in sod,
But do not cry for this man, son,
For he said there is no God."

At seventeen, he courted a wife
Though he had no bigger plan
To make bootlegging a family life.
He was a moonshine man.

His wife sewed shirts at the Factory[166].
He piddled here and there.
His kids at ages two and three
Got lice all in their hair.

When they shaved poor Bessie's head,
They found a tumor on her brain.
She lived her short life strapped in bed
Shriveled up in pain.

The Factory gave no insurance,
So he had to sell Ma and Pa's cabin
And all the rest of his inheritance
To pay for Bessie's medicine.

Before she died, he built her a casket
With maples sides and a white oak top,
At her funeral, he stank of whiskey,
Then never drank another drop.

Chorus:
I watched him live, and I watched him die,
And never, one time, heard him curse.
I witnessed many a deep felt sigh,
But hardly any worse.
Still, I turned away from his grave
With no teardrop in my eye
Until I heard a stranger say
As I was passing by,
"This man's sad lot in life is done

And they've covered him in sod,
But do not cry for this man, son,
For he said there is no God."

Little Johnny was nothing but trouble
And spoilt by his mama's hand.
By fourteen, he'd seen juvie hall,
By eighteen, the state pen.

There, he found a new obsession,
An all-forgiving savior.
After eighteen months for possession,
He was out on good behavior.

On Sundays, he carried his Mama to church,
Where she smiled and patted his hand.
They sat in the chain swing on the porch
And boomed out "Let's Take the Land."[167]

Johnny's work hours were pretty weird,
But he wore some fancy clothes.
He drove a souped-up Firebird
With really dark-tinted windows[168].

He was in the church when the doors were open.
When they weren't, he couldn't be found.
His daddy was certainly hopin'
He wasn't out jackin' around.

Johnny might have had his Mama fooled,
But not so much his dad,

Who shivered when little Johnny was killed
During a drug deal gone bad[169].

Chorus:
I watched him live, and I watched him die,
And never, one time, heard him curse.
I witnessed many a deep felt sigh,
But hardly any worse.
Still, I turned away from his grave
With no teardrop in my eye
Until I heard a stranger say
As I was passing by,
"This man's sad lot in life is done
And they've covered him in sod,
But do not cry for this man, son,
For he said there is no God."

With little Johnny buried, the wife would not survive.
Her heart was torn in pieces
Much too small for her to live
But still beating in the creases.

She got her a scrip for opies[170],
Paid for by Medicaid.
She spent her days all dopey
And sipping lemonade.

Ten years, she shuffled through the house
In a disconnected haze.
One day, he shook her lifeless form,
She'd been dead two or three days.

He buried her next to her son
In a grave far away from their daughter's.
To this day, she still has no stone
Only a gray metal marker[171].

Chorus:
I watched him live, and I watched him die,
And never, one time, heard him curse.
I witnessed many a deep felt sigh,
But hardly any worse.
Still, I turned away from his grave
With no teardrop in my eye
Until I heard a stranger say
As I was passing by,
"This man's sad lot in life is done
And they've covered him in sod,
But do not cry for this man, son,
For he said there is no God."

I knew ol' Harlan pretty well,
Bought his firewood and 'shine[172].
I carried his livestock to the sale
Whenever I took mine.

One time when I was short on luck
And feeling mostly alone,
He and I bought an Army surplus truck
And made money hauling stone[173].

He told me stories about a war[174],
Though I'd never known he'd served.
They were like no tales I'd heard before,
Harlan *always* lost his nerve.

He hid behind trees and hid in holes,
And he swore he never fired his gun.
Then, he showed me a handful of medals.
He never should've won.

Now, that's according to him not me,
I thought he was pretty smart.
I think we best serve our country
By not getting blown apart.

I guess that what I'm trying to say
Is that this man seemed my friend.
He never got in anyone's way
Nor had any fences to mend.

I don't know what he believed,
And I don't know what he thought.
I don't think that he was deceived
But I can't say that he was not.

Was he a good man? I don't know.
He did some illegal things.
He never hurt a human though
Or called anyone bad names.

His life was full of loss and hurt,
Cathead biscuits and bacon grease.
He was born to parents poor as dirt
And never knew a moment's peace.

Maybe he said, "There is no God,"
And maybe he was right.
I will not argue what he said or did,
But I think a real God might.

Chorus:
I watched him live, and I watched him die,
And never, one time, heard him curse.
I witnessed many a deep felt sigh,
But hardly any worse.
Still, I turned away from his grave
With no teardrop in my eye
Until I heard a stranger say
As I was passing by,
"This man's sad lot in life is done
And they've covered him in sod,
But do not cry for this man, son,
For he said there is no God."

Laocoön[175]

I.

Riding the dark waves' foamy crest,
Two serpents slither breast to breast,
Their fiery eyes and blazing breaths,
Concealed before the blood-red sun.
Across the twilight sands, they twist
Spreading foul poisons in the mist,
Keeping their god-appointed tryst.
Troy's soldiers drop their spears and run.

II.

A troubled father kneels in prayer,
His rites performed with priestly care.
His blood libations[176] fill the air
With tangs that hide the poison's scent.
On temple steps, two boys at play
Are in the god-sent serpents' way
And their sad fates upon this day
Were being where blind vengeance went.

III.

The father knows Achaean[177] spies
Lie waiting in that wicked prize.
Why will not Priam realize
He seals his reckless kingdom's doom?
What fools are Trojans to believe
That enemies dare not deceive
Through gifts to fickle gods they leave
When gods themselves would Troy consume.

IV.

Then, muffled cries reach baffled ears,
Sparking a father's deepest fears,
And from one sacrifice he tears
To find his sons martyred for Greece.
Cursing both fickle gods and men,
He rends his robe and charges in
To fight for lives he cannot win
Against two fiends who grant no peace.

V.

Still, try he must to break the grasp
And let his murdered children gasp
One breath of life before Death's clasp
Provides an infinite relief.
Although he's pierced by toxic fangs,
A needling guilt above him hangs
That stings him more than poison's pangs.
His children died for his belief.

VI.

Sobbing for breath and steeped in gore,
The doomed man writhes upon the floor,
Damning the gods who watch no more
This massacre of faultless youth,
For they know well the dying cries
Of newborn babes and widowed wives
Whose only sin is trusting lies
Revealed to them as father's truth.

VII.

Laocoön is now at rest,
His mangled boys clasped to his breast.
The monstrous snakes that killed them nest
At wise Pallas Athena's feet.
King Priam and the Trojans haul
The wooden horse into their mall
And praise the gods for Troy's great wall
That bested Agamemnon's fleet[178].

Suicide Notes[179]

My claws ache, and a lousy numbness pains
My legs as if Time were still mid-winter dim
And cold March mists, turned into icy rains,
Have frozen me fast to this crackling limb.
    I am affixed here by frigid sorrow
That wets my eyes in the early dawn light
And fractures Hope into glistening shards
    Of a broken tomorrow
Where nothing present in the world is right
Except the penned grief of long-dead bards.[180]

    Oh, for a novel notion not taken
By some self-anointed bird of mourning
    So all dull lyrics might re-awaken
With a boisterous, euphonic warning!
Now, I am a songster of somber note
With despondent tears obscuring his eye
And misery muting his gloomy hymn.
Oh, for a full-throttled chirruping throat,
    A bold, unburdened cry[181],
That I may fill each new verse to the brim!

Fill it with light and love *and quite forget*[182]
That devil-boy with his wrist sling shot
And an assorted steel ball-bearing kit.
He always misses, but not by a lot!
Damn, that sly snake that gobbles peeping chicks,
Slipping soundless and unseen through trees
That hide it in their devious green leaves!
I wish I could I ignore their wicked tricks
And the cold malicious ease
With which our gods create killers and thieves.

Thieves, whistling wildly to amorous hens,
Their puerile lines stealing prospective mates,
Burglars who pilfer with papers and pens
The interest of all our loves—and our hates—
Each one rending a transient delight
From the poet's veiled responsive soul,
Filching the muse for whom he writes or sings.
Ah, well! Try and do whatever they might,
They cannot mend the whole,
Nor can they bring an end to all good things.

I, though, I can force an end to it all.
Get away! I really will! I will jump!
Down, down where the ants look—well—very small,
I will crash an unyielding, muddled lump.
Taciturn on Mother Earth's cold, taut breast,
I will cast what once was Me all around
So that you cannot turn your callous eye
From my closing statement, my very best

Expression without sound.
But why should I die? By god, I can fly!

Fly away! Fly away! Oh, silly bird!
The old woman's scruffy cat is aprowl
And who knows whose warbles it may have heard
Or whose feathers will feed its throaty growl?
An egg-deserter sits on the birdbath
Listening to a lark announcing spring.
The cat has slowed into a noiseless stalk
And taps its padded paws upon the path.
Should I warn? Should I sing?
Or have portents of Death been but brave talk?

Talk, I think, only talk and nothing more.
Perhaps, I might learn a way to love life,
To listen to the modish birds who bore
Me with their egotistic inner strife,
And to adopt the broad atheist's view
That no gods control this boorish chaos,
The snake's raw hunger, or the savage cat.
I can come to terms with my sorrow too.
What soul has not known loss?
Even base villains suffer tit-for-tat[183].

Ah, yes, I suppose that I will jump now
That I have reasoned with my inner fears.
Leap and fly to light on a higher bough
Above the churning flood of selfish tears.
Listen—the hummingbirds buzz the bee balm,
The mourning doves' coos fill hazy green hills,

Tree to tree the tweeting titmouse races.
The chorus quickens all Nature's deep calm,
Cheeping, peeping, piping trills,
Echoing Life through Time's empty spaces.

The Purple Thistle[184]:
(Old #5)[185]

In the rustling breath of harvest twilight,
The purple thistle spreads its frosty leaves,
Grasping wisps of eastern silver sky light
And evanescent nips of Autumn eves[186]
Yet does not yield to peaceful sleep too soon
In the soothing aura of mother moon.

Held fast in fertile soil with heavy sigh,
Tall grasses wag their lush seeds in the wind,
Strewing for migrant birds a food supply
And tickling drowsy cows upon the chin
While twisting supple torsos to a tune
Pronounced in silence by the rising moon.

Black-eyed Susan[187] blooms bump Queen Anne's fine lace
Smearing sinless white licentious yellow.
A green grasshopper springs in empty space;
A sleek barn swallow stabs the poor fellow
And skitters to his nest with scratch-legged boon,
His sickle shadow on the bald-faced moon.

The thistle whispers in its zealous sleep
A savior's myth that whips through fervent dreams.
Bedecked in thorns and swathed in purple deep[188],
The thistle knows no suffering nor seems[189],
Its faith a tricky hieroglyph or rune
Translated by old lovers of the moon[190].

Now, both horizons blush a wounded red,
But neither orb bobs in a brightening sky.
The sleepy thistle rises from the dead
Or from a dream in which it cannot die.
The moon is gone; the sun razes the gray[191].
A farmer with a spray tank walks that way.

Assured it has no rot or leaf disease,
The flower flaunts its health and beams with pride.
The man believes it's just a weed he sees
And cures the nuisance with an herbicide.
From a brass nozzle, poison mists whistle
Crusting and killing the guiltless thistle.

Slender tan grasses bend in passive bows.
Tired winds weave lazy circles to nestle
Near the bristly noses of blissful cows
In a reformed field without one thistle.
They murmur and warble as if to croon
But sing no excuse to the chary[192] moon.[193]

Indifference[194]

(With deference to Matthew Arnold)

We grow more content year by year
In the comfort of modern life.
Great passion is the thing we fear,
The zealous root of all Man's strife.
We make our peace with tepid love,
For we have nothing left to prove.

We eat our mush that has no taste
And are happy it is not spiced.
Original thought is such a waste
When we prefer our white bread sliced.
White bread, white mush, and table salt,
The things we love! It's not our fault!

We're trained to think about a box,
To wrap our minds around a square.
What use is truth or paradox
When even faith is empty air?
And we can quickly heat faith up
As fast as we can eat it up?

Ah, the cynical soul of wit,
The greatest sense of irony,
Is valued near the same as spit
And slightly more than poetry.
For us, it is dressed for TV
And nimbly masked in comedy.

True to its form, no subject bores
Or holds our interest for less time
Than all of our incessant wars
And the political sublime.
By "sublime," I mean "religion,"
A matter too dull to mention.

Duller still are our feeble laws
And dimmer still the enforcers,
For what was once probable cause
Is now employment for lawyers
Who become the judges of peers
And stick blind justice in arrears[195].

But you and I, are we content
To let the others live as fools?
Is this the style in which we meant
To squander our poetic tools?
And could we set the world aright?
Well…probably not—but we might.

Lily

Lily loves a painted garden,
No pollen for her nose.
She knows an image, like a name,
Can smell of any rose[196].

Lily wants a lot of love,
But none that she can feel,
A lover who fills all her needs
With nothing that is real.

Lily lives a happy life
Ensconced upon a wall,
Embowered in a joy and peace
With no pain near at all.

But Lily is a bully
In a world she has not seen,
So Lily leads a lonely life
With a lovely little screen.

Lover Lost in Time

I.

The shade grows lucid with pale light,
And I chastise my blinking eyes
By closing their dark lids so tight
That even they don't realize
What it is they do not see,
Who it is committing a crime,
Who it is that has injured me
This last morning and this last Time.

II.

I lie here covered but still cold,
Where once her warmth did press my back,
And her loving limbs did enfold
Me with a fervor that I lack,
A zeal for life I cannot find,
A mystic sense of love sublime
That I sequester in my mind
And leave untroubled for all Time.

III.

Here is the pillow where her head
With long and lovely brown hair splayed
Like flames around her on the bed—
No, no—nor the curve her form made
In the mattress—it is not there!
No impression of her, but I'm
Pretty sure this one strand of hair
Has been lying here all this Time.

IV.

What silence! I hear the clock tick
As I might have heard her fond heart
Beat, slow in peaceful sleep and quick
As my morning mood made her start
With rough, scratchy, whiskered kisses.
Silence breaks with the cursed clock's chime
And foolish memory hisses
Away from all-destroying Time.

V.

I believe, soon, I will forget
The hours that my coarse hands caressed
The softness of her skin, and yet
I doubt I can forget the rest,
The story of a love so deep
It's only told in pantomime,
But lovers learn it when they leap
Into the path of fleeting Time.

VI.

Time, Time, that tells me she is gone!
Time, Time, that cannot tell me why!
Time, the master I counted on
To hold her slave to me, but I
Underestimated her will,
The purpose in the paradigm[197]
Of one who can but won't stay still
For any certain length of Time.

VII.

Time has passed. A shadow falls
Across my face and on my mind.
I watch it amble up the walls.
I stare at it until I'm blind.
I have not moved one inch all day
As I've watched a ghost rise and climb
From the pillow where she once lay
In a finer and faster Time.

Not Knowing If You Dream[198]

You moaned as thunder gathered in the air;
The muddled world outside rumbled and shook;
You straightened out beside my elbow's crook
But never even knew the storm was there.

You never felt my fingers brush your cheek
Nor saw the lightning fracture blackest night,
Nor did you know my poor heart skipped with fright
When, in the squall, a voice like Death did speak.

"See how she lies a corpse within a tomb,
And, but for trifling fantasies, at peace?
Her bliss will come when all her dreamings cease."
And then a chilly shade seeped in the room.

The dreadful haze weighed less than a minute
But left a deep impression on the place.
Your body clearly fills an empty space,
But where will you be with no dreams in it?

The sun cleared out a blindingly blue sky.
You yawned and stretched, crisscrossing all the bed,

Then turned to ask what thoughts traversed my head.
Not knowing if you dream, I had to lie.

A Seven-Hour Love Song[199]

The Prelude

The omniscient summer sun sneaks away
Into the scent of honey-suckled dew
And delusional mist of fresh mown hay,
Leaving its prescient guard o'er the day
Enfolding itself in a veil of blue.
Innocent offspring of water and sun
Fade also into the purple-grey hue
To sleep in the warmth of a day well done.

Soon, the shine on dusty hills has faded.
Crosstie fires arise like beacons of light,
Calling America's wild and jaded,
Moth-like into the mysteries of night.
Here, young lovers bend and sway, kiss and part
To twangy guitars and songs so sentimental
That sincerity is lost in the art.
For these youth, the words are incidental
As most trifles are that come from the heart.

9:00 PM

The firelight on his ruddy face
Covered every blemish and trace,
So he looked like a Lancelot[200]
Before the fall from Arthur's grace
When he charmed that gal from Shallot[201].
And Guinevere[202], now, she was hot!
With the fire gleaming brightly behind,
She was the image of Venus
Botticelli[203] might bring to mind,
But the lady in that scene is
Naked, and Gwen was surely not,
So, reader, put aside that thought.

She was no goddess; this is true,
But so heavenly in his eyes
That when she smiled at him, on cue,
His piety began to rise.

10:00 PM

The odor of love is ticklish
When wafting on a soft night's mist.
If he smells like lime and licorice[204],
No mortal woman can resist,
But even if he smells like beer
With a whisper of cigarette smoke,
The smell of love subdues all fear.
It did. He grinned. They met. She spoke.

11:00 PM

She said she was from Baton Rouge[205]
Here with some friends from the college
That Cajun boys were all just huge
Rubes—and other offhand knowledge.
He talked about his father's farm
Where more than childhood dreams are lost,
And then to show he had some charm,
He quoted her some Robert Frost.

Now, readers, this is not to say
That the young man knew his writers.
He had learned *Nothing Gold Can Stay*
From the movie *The Outsiders*,
Which is based upon a fine book[206]
That our Lance has not ever read.
I warn before you take a look
That poor Johnny Cade ends up dead.
Please forgive this lame digression,
It serves our lovers none too well,
And neither would learn a lesson
From the moral it has to tell.

The next few lines are not a quote,
But something like what Frost once wrote[207].

The words they spoke all lovers know
As seeds prospective partners sow.
They never think of stopping here

To till a plot where love can grow.

Yes, lover's schemes are somewhat queer
To love what's far and not what's near
As if one night, for Cupid's sake,
Could fill an absence of a year.

A Nazareth song gave them a shake
And warned them of that big mistake,
Yet each heart was willing to weep
For love that one long night could make.

"Love hurts, love scars," and love wounds deep,
And promises are hard to keep
And prices lovers pay are steep
In restless nights of aching sleep.

What? "Nazareth?" you say? Why, yes.
The lyrics work excellently
"Some fools fool themselves, I guess;
They're not foolin' me."
Phil and Don did sing the song first.
My mind is not lost in a fog.
Before you think my taste the worst,
Do remember "Hair of the Dog." —

So…our lovers meet though forewarned
That their path may lead to sorrow,
But, oh! With night, so well adorned
Who can care about tomorrow?

12:00 AM

The songs that crackle from the radio
To mingle in the midnight fog
And seep through the valley below,
Are imitations, don't you know,
Of the *Concerto des Bullfrog*—
A lot of noise with nothing said
But hard to get out of your head.

She sidled near; he dropped his beer
And ran to the cooler for more.
When he moved there, she shifted here,
But accidentally, for sure.

Each of the lovers played a part
In contrast to the other's turns,
Not of the mind but of the heart.
Level-headedness never yearns.

The soundless waves of moonbeams splash
On senselessly smiling faces.
If shyness wanes, they still may crash,
But coy hands have other places
To hide like handy front pockets.

Whether stoned on love, beer, or grass,
The pounding darkness quaked too much
To let another tremor pass.

His hand and hers were forced to touch.
Sparklers! Spinners! Pinwheels! Rockets!

1:00 AM

Only the drunks keep lovers company,
Staggering, reeling, pressing much too close.
Some flirt with wit, but few are too canny
To the fact that they are verbose.

Into the shadowed dampness, they
Escape past trucks with squeaky springs,
Past cars where awkward lovers play,
Past Paul McCartney and the Wings,
I'm only telling what is so.
Past skin squeaking a vinyl seat,
Past quickly discarded panties,
Past the druggies sampling a treat
That causes an ache it can't ease.

Down on the glowing, pebbled bank,
Near the quivering, moonlit stream,
Our hopeless, helpless lovers shrank
Into the arc of one small beam.

2:00 AM

Down on the bank, on the gravel,
They sat to sort their feelings through,
But half-baked plans soon unravel
Fastened only with hunger's glue.

With his body, he formed a chair,
And in this comfort she reclined.
His heart was tangled in her hair,
His breath was messing with her mind.

While stars fell from the sky, they talked.
While mists rose from the creek, they sat.
When passion smothered sighs, they walked
Till neither knew where they were at.

When skin touches skin, souls shiver
More from the heat than from the cold.
With one caress, couples quiver
If either one would be so bold.

The moonlight dancing on clear streams
Lets wavelets clasp the beam and sway.
A kiss is easy, so it seems,
Unless the lips are far away.

While waters dance, urges ripple.
He thought he felt her brush his thigh.
The zephyr brushing her nipple
Was stirring moisture in her eye.

She felt a hardness touch her back;
She coyly bent to fix her sock,
But when she yielded and leaned back,
He somehow had removed the rock.

He whispered, "I can wait for you."
Her body tensed as though the door
Was opened now to let him through.
In fact, it was her butt was sore
From sitting there an hour or two
And she could stand to sit no more
Without some sign of what to do.

No accident nor stroke of luck
Seemed destined to unite this pair.
It was quite clear they would not pluck
Carnal contact out of the air.

Platonic love blooms where it may.
If he had kissed her, she'd have come
Around to a more sensual way,
But as it was, her legs were numb,
So she could neither come nor stay
And to her needs he was too dumb.

3:00 AM

Poisonous Sun! Bane of Lovers!
Let love brew beneath night's covers.
They've not had time to seize their piece.
They require still a moment's lease

To let dear Venus teach their hearts
To move on to the other parts—

Body parts, like lips and fingers
On necks and breasts and inner thighs.
Where touches burn, the heat lingers
And dissolves into hungry sighs.

And all of this so close, so near,
Guide his hand, Gwen, take it in yours,
Cause his lips to caress your ear,
Don't let his shyness shape the course
Of the greatest love you may know.
Time flies while he wrestles with fear,
The concern that you might say, "No!"
Carpe Diem[208]! Or this one night,
Create a love to fill your dreams,
This man, this boy, this country sprite
Can be the fantasy he seems
And then live on in memory,
Forever bright as what can be
And never tarnished with what is.
Make him a dream and become his.

Well, my chance to warn is long gone.
This story is many years old,
And my advice must be withdrawn;
The hottest fire leaves ashes cold,
And though it may refine the gold,
The metal from its ore is drawn.
No substances do the flames hold.
And yet there is more to be told,
Before we quit, before the dawn.

Though after three, the Sun still sleeps,
But up the quiet creek, light creeps.
The couple, who will curse their luck,
Are trapped in the lights of a truck.

With engine roaring, speakers loud,
The revelers rend the peaceful shroud
That cloaks the lovers in the night.
Out of the clamor comes a shout,
And a drunken girlfriend spills out,
"Hey! Hey! Ish everything alright?"
The end is near! I see, but hope
This storyteller is no dope.
A poet of love worth a piss
Won't leave his verse without one kiss[209].

And yet, of things one may describe,
A kiss is best to circumscribe.
For that which might be said is wrong.
Too many words leave little tongue.

Lips reach and mouths open slightly,
Necks crane like accepting a noose,
Hands clasp eager hips so lightly,
The pounding of hearts shakes them loose.
Eyes close as if acting asleep,
Noses seek out a route to one side,
(How awkward when both turn the same!)
Through dampened lips, probing tongues creep
As ravenous mouths open wide,
(Did you think that the kiss would be tame?)

Finally, arms pull bodies close,
Hands find those sensitive places
That only kisses can expose.
One rough finger gently traces,
The curvature under her breast.
She slides her hand down his belly,
And—readers can assume the rest—
All four legs quivered like jelly.

Kisses, though brief, live forever
When wet lips turn now into never
And never's the same as timeless.
(Some think I'm just being clever,
But without "never" I'm rhymeless.)

Time might be fixed, but it will fly
And soar unfettered to the end.
The kiss is endless but "Goodbye,
I really must go with my friend."

"Good-bye! Good-bye! Call me real soon."
"Good-bye! Good-bye! Be back in June."
Promises! Promises! But why
Are there no tears in any eye?

7:00 PM, August 31, That Same Year

"Hey, Lance, this is Dawn returning your call.
Gwen took a vacation early this fall
And didn't have time to come back around.
She wanted me to tell you she has found
A new friend who, uh…goes to college here.
She is going to have a busy year,
So don't be hurt if she forgets to call.
Maybe she can come up with me this fall.
We might party again if we can come.
Gotta go now,"—then the long distance hum.

He went to the couch and sat by a girl
Who wistfully twisted a reckless curl.
It took some time for the question to dawn,
At least until a commercial was on.
"Who was that?" she asked, but got no reply.
"It's better," he thought, "To ignore than lie."
So, he ignored in her arms all that night,
And only lied once before the dim light,
But many dreams tell him what has been lost
In that long summer before killing frost.

The End of Love

(A Just Song)

Just stop! We should not quarrel anymore.
You do as you wish, and I will move on.
Both will manage just the same as before,
But you will be here and I will be gone.
Just admit we were fooled by Love's fragrance,
A soothing scent that set our thoughts aswoon,
We were lulled by a dainty lovers' dance
In soft-sighing winds under a stirring moon.
I do not quarrel, but did we not think
About our future shackled side by side,
How each crashing wave causes both to sink
When either soul's sucked under by the tide?
Your love will not sustain me when I drown;
I do not need you near when I go down.

The Ghost of Marcellus[210]

Can I believe at all in one's belief
Who sees enlightened day in murky night,
Who bears self-evidence in such relief
That what he claims is always out of sight?
But with so many watchers gathered here,
It should be very clear what's true is true,
And though some aberrations do appear,
One can't deny what's seen by more than two.

Some honest persons must speak to these themes,
For ghosts do thrive when gullible men rule
And answers to questions are all in "seems"
When figures float through the thoughts of a fool.

Please, step up now, who has wit to explain
How fearing strangers fosters making friends,
When standing for values implies to complain,
Why lies can serve as a means to all ends,
How people make peace while practicing war,
Why Christians divide and think they can stand,
As God commands, for the orphans and poor
While letting false prophets sully their land?

Does the sun shine at night or moon in day?
Who is it will tell? Who knows what to say?

What reason can burst this sack of hot air?
What charm can remove this self-loving curse,
For its skin is thick as its iron hair
And stirring the stench just makes the smell worse?

Now, time is ticking away on the clock
But times will surely change, and truth will sing,
And sluggish seconds do the seasons mock,
But reason, like the hour, yet will ring.
Hope will replace the deep feelings of dread,
Sense will supplant the rantings of the mad
And light will shine when all by love are led.
Instead of those who find their lives "so sad."

Do that, I pray, and every morning know,
That finding truth is knowing where to go.

A New Woman with No Fear

Part 1: My Muse Is My Own

Inside a dull, disordered mind,
There are no drafts for memory.
Snippets fly and float about
And one of those drifted by me.

Chance can hardly concede the cause,
For I was reading my first book,[211]
One that I do not care for much,
But, if you've time, it's worth a look.

I flipped through pages, marking how
Both childish faiths and fears do flee,
And then amidst the false pretense
A gem of truth shined out at me.

I can love a woman when she has no fear.[212]

These words were written in rough lines
And rustic thoughts not studied much
And scattered in discordant rhyme

Lacking a careful craftsman's touch.

The story, it was not well told,
The verses, not quite lyrical,
But knowing that the gist was real
Made it quite less chimerical[213].

The stage exists, the people too
Though many have left their places,
Now, I, the remote manager,
Will refill the empty spaces.

Past twenty years or maybe more,
The images I sense and see,
And maybe now, mature, aloof,
I'll reconstruct the memory[214].

Part 2: What Am I Doing?

In '98, I often spent
My afternoons at Blanchard Springs[215].
My sons, most days, accompanied me,
But they were doing other things.

I took a cooler full of ice,
One ribeye steak, a case of beer,
Charcoal briquettes and paper plates...
Whatever else is not so clear.

But now, I pause to wonder why
I think details should be precise.
Suffice to say, on that one day
I had raw meat and beer on ice.

I was alone in Nature pure
Beneath the bough of virgin pine,
Each rounded hill and jutting rock,
A future memory of mine.

The crystal springs and Mirror Lake,
Pretending it can be blue sky,
Are part of me and all from me
No matter where my mind does lie.

A picnic site close to the bridge
Was the center of these places
Where I could grill and drink my beer
And tend my soul's empty spaces.

I was alone or so I thought
With no notion but the hush
Of water trickling over rocks
And balmy breezes in the brush.

The hard, black coals had heated white,
The steak's first side was seared,
When on a trail from out the woods,
A small girl on a bike appeared.

Part 3: "Wherefore art thou going, Child?" Or Something Like That?

She coasted down a packed-dirt path
Through timber of primal sublime
Riding a rusty Huffy bike
That had been pink upon a time.

The dirt trail turned to sidewalk
In the clearing nearest me.
She pedaled hard on down the hill
Where she came to an offset tee,

And when she rode out of my sight
Down near the shelter bluff,
I turned to see if my thick steak
Had been browned by the fire enough.

Part 4: A Steak Interrupted

It had! And it was tender too!
A meaty morsel fit for gods,
But who would offer flesh to them
Is a cult of sacrificial clods.

Ice, cold beer, and fat, sizzling steaks
Are victuals[216] that make gods of men.

I sliced the first succulent bite,
And there's that little girl again.

Part 5: "Send in the Nuns!"[217]
Not Quite

I nodded with my hands both full.
She didn't even try to wave.
I guess that on this second pass
She could not risk being that brave.

But I saw on her smiling face
Her fear was steadily fleeting
And knew next time that when she passed
I'd receive a bolder greeting.

She worked her pedals hard again
And eased into a stable glide
Then swerved to miss a white church bus
With a flaming red cross on its side.

The bus was really not that close,
But it was something new,
A novel pawn in our strange game
That caused me a divergence too.

A dozen women rallied out,
Many younger than you would think
Would be day-tripping with a church.
And some were dressed to draw a wink

Or a blink, a nod, or a stare.
So I opened my second beer
And watched the tempting church ladies
Unload a ton of pious gear.

A tablecloth, a canopy,
A container of utensils,
Some other tubs of God-knows-what,
White paper and colored pencils.

As I surveyed through mirrored shades,
This gal in a blue swimming suit
Kept casting furtive glances my way
As Eve had eyed the serpent's fruit[218].

"Lady," I said inside my head,
"Don't think that I'd ask you to stray.
I'm here to spend some time alone
And leave here in much the same way."

I thought more as I cleaned the grill
How I could gently turn her down,
But when I turned back from my task,
New Eve was no longer around.

Part 6: And Neither Was the Girl on the Bike

Now where is that girl on the bike?
She has been gone for quite a while.
The circle 'round the field and back
Is no more than a quarter mile.

She surely should be back by now…
But would she have gone on the road?
And why is that my business?
I guess I am in "father-mode."

Surely, she has a mother near
And maybe a father as well,
And everyone is eating lunch
As near and far as I can smell.

That is the way I was thinking
As I swabbed my sunblock on
And then my addled attention
Was drawn by a game on the lawn.

Part 7: An Even Stranger Game

On the sunny side of the field,
Two couples had put up a net
And started to play the strangest match
That I have tried to picture yet.

Now, I have seen and played the game
It is simply called "volleyball,"
But what they played within the game
Was hardly the same game at all.

First, I must be Homer[219], I guess
And put my combatants in arms
But somehow with much fewer words
On warriors with much lesser charms.

The women—How can I say this?—
Were very well put together.
They had the clothing and the gear
That perfectly suited the weather.

Their hair was pulled back tight in tails,
Visors shaded their painted eyes,
Sportswear compressed their tiny breasts
And compacted their skinny thighs.

They wore elbow pads on their arms
And padded braces on their knees.
Their shoes and socks revealed name brands

Evoking ancient victories.

Their bronze skins were lightly oiled
With a sweat-free sunblock lotion.
Their movements unlike their branding
Were not poetry in motion.

The men, well, I don't remember,
But one was beet-red on his back.
They both wore beards and close-cropped hair
And one of them, of course, was "Jack."

The women posed on the one side;
The men played fools on the other,
The women set up like startled cats,
The men like Puck[220] and his brother.

The ball was served over the net.
The men whiffed at it with smiles.
The girls dove hard into the grass
But missed the ball by miles.

It was a most pathetic game
Without a save, a spike, or kill,
But it wasn't a lack of effort
Supplying the absence of skill.

I do not know if the men saw the ball
On most of the service passes,
They were too busy bumping chests,
High-fiving, and slapping asses.

Their hands, all over each other,
Hardly ever struck the ball
While the women on the other side
Never touched anything at all.

Oh, there were certain exchanges
With a product or hair out of place
And many a time-out was taken
To tweak and adjust a knee brace.

While each man played with the other,
Each woman performed on her own,
Looking so poised and well-polished,
Like manikins carved out of stone.

Ugh! I have let my beer get warm,
Watching this peculiar display.
Where has the girl on the bike gone?
Will she be back over this way?

Part 8: Bored with Old Games

All my trash had been placed in bins
Everything else back in the truck
Except for my chair and the cooler
And—Oh! No! I curse the bad luck!

A woman I'd known since grade school
Whose crushes I'd managed to flee
Was setting up lunch on the table
In the picnic site next to me.

She was surrounded by sisters
And children from tots to teens.
She wore a black bikini top
And old faded cut-off jeans.

Her glowing tan came from a can.
Her ample breasts swung left to right
As she bent over picnic wares
To make sure that I could see white.

And I did from top to bottom,
For she flashed for my shaded eyes
Her creamy cheeks and shaved nethers
As she rubbed lotion on her thighs.

I say that this show was for me.
No men were around there who might
Be tempted to sample the treasures
So purposely put in my sight.

I guess I looked. How could I not
With an amused curiosity?
How much was she willing to bare
And what did she think I would see?

A pleasure that I could not pass?
An offer I could not forbear?
A jackpot that required no tax?
A friendly bait without a snare?

I beheld a hopeless amour
That would end exactly the same
As it had every time before this day
In her tiresome flirtatious game.

Part 9: Off to the Water
with the Rest of the Animals

So I put my chair in its bag
A swig of cold beer in my cheek,
Hoisted a half-empty cooler
And headed on down to the creek

Where all the animals gathered
For either pastime or repose,
To play in the chilly water
Or sun on the bank in small clothes.

I chose to do the former,
So I swam to the other side
And sat on a rock, still neck deep,
When up on the beach side I spied

The little girl from the bicycle
A woman, maybe her mother,

And a tot with arm rings on
Who could only be her brother.

She recognized me instantly
And threw up her hand in a wave
With no balance to be maintained,
She certainly could be brave.

I returned her bold attention
With a wave of my hand, but then
Wondered if I should be flirting
With a girl who was nine or ten.

I don't think that it is flirting
To pay well-mannered attention
With anything but courtesy
At the heart of good intention.

Then, another thought bothered me
Like a fly buzzing at my ear,
Why she was the only female
Whose actions, to me, seemed sincere?

Part 10: The Answer Presents Itself

I looked up and down the swimming hole
At the women who'd come to play
At sunning, swimming, or resting
On this exquisite August day.

There were lots of different sorts
In sundry ages, moods, and sizes,
But among the whole assortment,
There were very few surprises.

Some feared their kids waded too deep,
Some feared the wrath of the sun,
Some worried they were too exposed,
And some were afraid to have fun.

All seemed to feel others watching
And, thus, they feared being judged
Of their worth as mothers and women,
Of their characters being smudged.

Other doubts I might have noted
Had I time to study the place,
But the plunk of a projectile
Splashed cold water onto my face.

I turned to see the bike rider
Hurling stones directly at me,
Most were landing far away,
But some came near dangerously.

"Hey, now! We don't throw rocks." I said,
"That is not a nice thing to do."
"Never fear," she answered in truth,
"I am not throwing them at you."

Still, it seemed I was the target
As her tosses went far and wide
Until I finally realized
She couldn't hit me if she tried.

She wasn't trying, she was playing,
And I just happened to be here.
She cared not what I was or thought
This modern woman with no fear.

Youth and Age

(A Nod to STC)[221]

I.

On this, your dying bed, I miss you more
Than I will ever have the strength to show
Or impart to you as I did before
When we were hungry poets and did grow
Spirit, body, and notions tightly twined.
The rapturous celebration of hair,
Eyes, limbs, and lips, the healthy decadence,
That we, in puerile candor, loved to share
We've set aside, and now I am inclined
To claim our youthful acts as ignorance.

II.

The songs that were not written are the best.
At least that's what we think. We set the bar
Extremely low, and without proof attest,
The rhymes are so much better than they are.
Now, I fear, as a rattle shakes your breath
And emptiness crawls across your dim eyes,
That all our finest ditties will be lost
To the wordless murmurs of long lost sighs

And that the sole lamenter of your death
Will bury the songs with you at great cost.

III.

And what happy songs! With no stiff charge
Except, perhaps, an unintended smile,
Or, when effortless rhythm was at large,
Some charming condemnation of our style.
It was all a joke and played for laughs.
Those laughs too, absorbed in the jagged beat,
Were gifts we wasted. The words we employed
Are gone with those happy, simple, and sweet
Poems of which no first or final drafts
Are left to puzzle over—or avoid.

IV.

I come to visit this decisive hour
Barely the shadow of a fellow priest[222],
Yet inspired by the prospective power
Of a higher wisdom to be released.
Knowledge must come; it must come at the end!
The Truth must be the damp pulp in the cup[223].
Here, sip, but leave a drop, one drop, for me.
You have no further need to lap it up
When you can leave it with your living friend
And not drag it into eternity.

V.

Don't think that I've reformed my fickle mind
Because my Art appears to want you gone;
I'll bury the poems you leave behind

As though they are but dead words of my own.
On to eternity, Childlike Poet,
And take with you this rude generation
Of conceited dealers of selfish woe.
No friends to Man nor imagination
Are they—and right damned eager to show it[224]!—
That thing that we were, I no longer know.

Ode on a Lizard and
a Lost Tale[225]

I.

Lizard of stripes, green, blue, and corn yellow,
Devotee of the early morning sun,
Dips and prays, a pious little fellow,
Then prowls when his devotionals are done.
He wriggles slowly through the creeping phlox
And slithers in the slime of dewy grass.
He nabs a kipping cricket off its guard
To break the lean hours of his nightly fast,
Then nimbly skips across a strip of rocks
To crawl beneath a ragged cardboard box
I carelessly left lying in the yard.

II.

How often do I see him? Every day?
Or only when I've time to weed the bed
Of irises where he so often lay?
Do I shake the excess soil on his head?
Is that what sends him rushing off so fast?
Has he acquired a sense of modesty?
—A trait most unproductive in a male

When courting counts on smug pomposity—
That shames him off into the unmown grass?
I did see something different our last pass.
The gaudy boy no longer has a tail!

III.

He has a stump where once he had a whip
And seems starkly diminished by the loss.
He left it hanging on a barn cat's lip
Like a blue and squirming dental floss.
It will grow back, my friend, no need to fear;
The simple often lose important parts.
Nothing in my liberal education
Or my deep knowledge of creative arts
Has ever taught me how in language clear
That he can make his lost limb reappear.
I doubt it requires imagination.

IV.

Without imagination, art is lost.
Without his tail, he is no pretty thing,
And recreation's bound to have a cost
No different for a lizard than a king,
Which calls to mind Jim Morrison of The Doors,
The "Lizard King" who lost his soul somewhere,
—Or maybe, I should say he lost his name[226]—
Whichever way, I really do not care,
But THIS distraction of my thinking pours
My best ideas to the abyss in scores,
And now my tale has vanished just the same.

V.

Vanished, like you my little lizard friend,
How quickly you can hide in empty space!
I will not look for you, let's not pretend,
When you are lost in any shady place.
Like words go AWOL[227] in a tangent thought
And good stories are wrecked in banal acts,
Like many loves are lost in misplaced mail
And many truths buried beneath the facts,
Some ballads disappear in themes they sought.
Before a minstrel brags on what he's caught,
Perhaps he should see if he's lost his tale.

No Empty Spaces

Art defines neither right nor left,
No demon's ditch[228] nor Yahweh's cleft[229],
No spring, no summer, no fall, nor winter
But stays confined in the center.
Equiponderant[230], I suppose,
Much like the petals on a rose.

Some pedants and sophists[231] have said,
Not understood but poorly read,
—And what they say is trivial at best—
That the center cannot be held[232],
Seen, tasted, heard, or smelled,
But exists in mental twinges
That occur along the fringes.
"We all know you're out there.[233]"

Their abstract forms pretend to move
As madness near the edge
While herding in a well-worn groove
Like rabbits through a hedge.
Peering into this false abyss[234],
They seem amazed to find

A mirror of the funfair[235] kind.
And who might its reflection be?
Why, it is either them or me?

Then, they age, and their hopes leave;
Their politics and passions change.
The glass exists but to deceive
And makes their own faces seem strange[236].
Give it a try! Come touch this page!
It is quite true, and it is firm,
But proves an ineffective berm
Against the surge of empty space.

Their simple thoughts lack ample width
To pilot them through time and space
And so they place the classic myth
Inside their own conceited place.
Their egos occupy their sleep
And imbue every night,
In tints of black and white,
Wave on wave of tumbling nothing,
Fantasies forged by idiots[237].

Art is not in the empty space.
It is in the infinite sky.
It conjures every mote and trace
Reflected on the mind and eye.
It sings of relevant things,
Of memories and gods,
Of atheists and kings,

Of chances and their odds,
And it does not care who listens.

Seething with life in subdued time,
Holding the best of day and night,
Art seeks a reason and a rhyme
To blush the dark and dim the light,
To sing in spring,
To welcome the winter,
To dance with bees upon the rose
And entice them to the center.
It's most sublime, I do suppose,
When it tells us what Nature knows.

My Son, My Poem[238]

I cast you off a thing of shame,
I cry you out for none to hear,
I give to you my humble name,
And then I call you back for fear

That I have left you half undone,
That you are only middling formed,
That I should send some perfect son,
So that the world is not alarmed

At the distortion of your start
And the discordance of your voice.
Because you are my only art,
I surely have no other choice.

Go, deliver my sad excuse
As witness to a timid heart
And suffer not the sure abuse
That's given you for my coy part.

Endnotes

[1] This poem is actually quite different than its original form. I noticed the original poem was similar in theme to Blake's *Introduction to Song of Innocence*, so I shaped my poem to imitate his form. I had to do a lot of cutting and, I think, made my poem better.

[2] This character was originally Da Vinci's Vitruvian man. He represents the art of the past. However, try fitting *Vitruvian* into a metrical scheme. It is not easy.

[3] Essentially, the past had nothing to do with me, but I am already influenced by it—in my heart. Ironically, I cannot leave it alone. It is me.

[4] The feminine aspects of the masculine personality: The goddess that remains in patriarchal religions.

[5] Any substance or idea that causes numbness or lack of awareness

[6] Like Coleridge's "poor nigh-related guest," old age

[7] This poem has been revised and re-written so many times that I cannot even say how many anymore. The influences in it are also so many that I cannot remember them all. It takes its "parts" from Eliot's *The Wasteland* and parodies,

imitates, or was inspired by that poem in many places though it is not intended, overall, as a parody.

[8] Referring to Cain, the first murderer, who killed his brother Abel and was cursed with exile.

[9] One of many references to the prophet and book of *Isaiah*. An angel touched his lips with a coal from the altar and his sins were removed.

[10] Pretty much the opposite of what Alexander Pope says in *An Essay on Criticism*

[11] A mimicry of Whitman's *I Sing the Body Electric*

[12] Previous three lines and some following allude to Eliot's *The Lovesong of J Alfred Prufrock*

[13] Painter known for *Self Portrait in a Convex Mirror*, the subject of John Ashbery's poem of the same name.

[14] Socrates and Alexander Pope

[15] The abuse of a thing does not deny its use: Words and ideas are often abused, but they sure are useful for communicating and for poetry.

[16] "I am not as I was" from Horace's *Odes: Book 4*

[17] The "lying on the side" in the next few lines alludes to the prophecies of Ezekiel in Chapter 4 of the prophet's book in the Old Testament.

[18] A female demon who has sex with a sleeping man to steal his seed

[19] "Out of the eater, something to eat; out of the strong, something sweet" Judges 14:14

[20] Jael, wife of Heber, drove a tent stake through the forehead of the Canaanite commander Sisera. Judges 4:21

[21] Moses made this bronze viper so that Hebrew who had been bitten by snakes would live by looking at it. Numbers 21:9

[22] Salome asked for the head of John the Baptist on a platter according the *Gospel of Mark*, Chapter 6. Some paintings portray the platter as silver.

[23] "My God! My God!" According to the *Gospel of Matthew*, Jesus cried these words on the cross. Some translations include "Why have you forsaken me?"

[24] In Acts 17, Paul tells the people of Athens that their unknown god is the God of the Jews.

[25] According to Matthew 26:13, Judas Iscariot betrayed Jesus for this amount.

[26] "She" is Venus de Milo. I have no idea how her lips are moist.

[27] A parody of Luke 7:36-50

[28] A self-contradictory statement that might sound true until reason is applied.

[29] The painting that I had in mind with this image is Ed Miracle's *I Told You So*. I wish that I could tell you where I saw the painting.

[30] "Tit for tat" means to do something annoying or unpleasant to someone because the person has done the same thing to you. Obviously, I am playing with its meaning a bit.

[31] Calling to mind *The Fire Sermon* from Eliot's *The Wasteland* and the Fire Sermon of Buddha, my "sermon" imitates Jesus' *Sermon on the Mount* from Matthew Chapter 5.

[32] Thomas Stearns Eliot

[33] Linter is the fuzz on a cotton seed after it has been through the gin.

[34] I am referring to the sea monster that "the Lord" hooks, hangs, grants mercy, makes an agreement with, toys with, and trades in Job 40:25-30

[35] I am the second Thomas, but I am also near-sighted, so maybe T.S Eliot and I swap places.

[36] Dante writes in *The Inferno*:
"As one Who vers'd in geometric lore, would fain Measure the circle; and, though pondering long And deeply, that beginning, which he needs, Finds not; e'en such was I, intent to scan The novel wonder, and trace out the form, How to the circle fitted, and therein How plac'd: but the flight was not for my wing; Had not a flash darted athwart my mind, And in the spleen unfolded what it sought."

[37] These quoted words and lines and the following themes are almost direct commentary on *The Wasteland: V: What the Thunder Said*

[38] The Gospel of John Chapter 5 talks of a "Sheep-Pool" in a place called Bethesda in which a person can be healed when the water is disturbed or moved, presumably by an angel.

[39] I simply mean to substitute one potential fact with another one that may signify the opposite idea.

[40] Isaiah 55:8

[41] The personification of utter confusion. I also like the old meaning of "with a yawning or gaping mouth."

[42] Kellie and I enjoyed the HBO series *Carnivále* by creator Daniel Knauf. The title is a tribute to that show.

[43] A small pointed or projecting part; also part of a pen

[44] I mean mysterious or magical objects or symbols

[45] Ratt is a "hair-metal" band who were popular in the 1980's.

[46] The chorus of the song fits the tone of the poem particularly well:

"Round and round With love we'll find a way just give it time Round and round What comes around goes around I'll tell you why"

[47] Childish or juvenile

[48] I realize now that I have answered Pink Floyd's question, "What shall we use to fill the empty space?" in the album *The Wall*.

[49] The grave is gelded because the body in it has lost a natural or essential part, mainly life.

[50] This poem mimics John Donne's *Song* or *Go and Catch a Falling Star*.

[51] "Maker" is a medieval term for poet.

[52] A chapbook is often less than 40 pages, so dancing on it spine would be pretty difficult. As related to poetry, a chapbook is a relatively cheap way for a poet to "publish" rather than through a publication house. Some people claim that chapbooks are more artistic because they are controlled by the artist. I say that chapbooks let most anyone claim to be a published poet.

[53] I cannot tell you how sick I am of reading and hearing of poets who take their "rhythms" from jazz. What a cop-out.

Jazz, which is really only good when it sounds like pop music, has varying rhythms like any other genre. Not having a regular rhythm in poetry is not like jazz; it is simply without rhythm.

[54] Italicized lines and words are taken straight from *St. Agnes' Eve*

[55] The two main characters in *St Agnes' Eve*

[56] In *Romeo and Juliet*, Mercutio tells the story of how Queen Mab infects dreams.

[57] Prophyro somehow treats Madeline with all kinds of tasty foods and drink.

[58] To be a true succubi, she must cause him to spill his seed. Here not to breed demons but to remind him of his failure, which perhaps does breed demons.

[59] A 1931 painting by Salvador Dalí. depicting, among other things, the warping of time.

[60] The boatman in Hades who ferried dead souls across the river Styx and Acheron.

[61] Here a key, but also a symbolic reminder of things revered mostly from the past

[62] One of my greatest literary inspirations has been John Keats poetic fascination with dreams. I often go where he went. However, as alluded to in the title of Part One, I can be more graphic with the sexuality than he could in his day.

[63] A mimicry of the last lines of *Ode to a Nightingale*

[64] Louis Comfort Tiffany created a well-known type of stained glass associated with the Art Nouveau and Aesthetic movements in art.

[65] A glass art technique in which colored glass is set in a pattern of concrete or epoxy resin

[66] A single color decoration, usually gray, used to produce a three dimensional effect

[67] Matte is generally without reflection. It is dull and lusterless. Her light changes that.

[68] Most readers assume that the message was sent to Time or Old Age. I can go along with that although I am not sure that was my original intention. I think I meant pretty much any negative or destructive thing or idea.

[69] This poem was inspired by the various presentations of Prometheus in painting. Prometheus stole fire from the gods of Olympus to enlighten mankind. His actions led to Pandora's box being opened and spilling all manner of evil onto the world, but also giving Hope to man. Prometheus was punished for his theft by being chained to a rock where his liver is consumed by vultures every day.

[70] Many philosophers, bolstered by modern psychological and behavioral studies, maintain that humans are so constrained by their environment and mental and nervous activities that freedom is merely an illusion. Other philosophers maintain that this "illusion" is enough, and Sartre famously said that we are always free to die.

[71] The very thing, poetry, that allows me to freely express myself also constrains me through the poets and critics past and present who tell me how I must do it to be accepted as a poet. I suspect, though I do not know, that dancers feel the same way.

[72] The title of this poem is ironic. Most people would assume that the carpenter is Jesus. However, many of the things that I have read say that the Greek term *tekton* used to describe Jesus' occupation would be better interpreted as craftsman or manual laborer.

[73] "Scaffold" has the dual meaning of both a supporting framework and a place where criminals are executed.

[74] Though the subject is quite controversial, Washington, Franklin, Jefferson, Quincy Adams, Madison, Paine, and Ethan Allen are but a few of the founding fathers who seemed to follow the deistic model of religion.

[75] The idea that there is an organized persecution of Christianity in the United States is ludicrous to me. The more evangelical a Christian denomination is the greater their persecution complex, it seems.

[76] With only a bit of exaggeration regarding the details of this story, most of it is relatively true. For instance, there is a Steffen creek but no Steffen bridge.

[77] Also, the Wilson girls were closer to my dad's age than mine, but I am assured that in their heyday they drew the young men like a shoofly pie draws flies.

[78] When Polyphemus, the cyclops, asked Odysseus his name so that he would know who had blinded him, Odysseus slyly gives his name as "Noman." Thus, when Polyphemus's neighbors ask why he is crying so loudly, he blusters, "Noman has blinded me," and they do not offer to help him. Shortly after this episode, Odysseus encounters the sirens who lure sailors to their deaths on the rocks and

also the sorceress Circe who lures men to her lair and kills them or turns them into animals.

[79] Oh, also, I never met Little Maggie McClain, but she does, or did, exist.

[80] How I came to be acquainted with Little Maggie and why I helped her with her mother's stuff is a story to be made up at a different time (See note above).

[81] Just so everyone is clear, I have never seen any letters or notes written by Kris Kristofferson though I spent an afternoon with him one time at the Brown Hole on Turkey Creek on Tony Joe White's property. Mr. Kristofferson watched my friend, Glenn Hicklin, and me perform stunts on a rope swing over the creek while he, Mr. White, and some guy I never knew drank whiskey straight from the bottle.

[82] All of the following quoted words are from songs that Kris Kristofferson wrote. Some of them are not the exact words nor are they in the exact order. Maggie's "letter" changes many of the words of *Me and Bobbie Mcgee*. The songs are (a test of my memory) *Help Me Make It Through the Night*, *For the Good Times*, *Sunday Morning Coming Down*, and *Me and Bobbie Mcgee*.

[83] The narrator of Poe's *The Raven* seeks surcease of sorrow in his "quaint and curious volume of forgotten lore."

[84] I have never read a letter written by Big Maggie McClain, and I also do not think that Kris Kristofferson wrote *Me and Bobbie Mcgee* about anybody. I am pretty sure that I have read that Bobbie McKee was the name of some producer's or writer's secretary.

[85] An apology follows.

[86] The two poets whose lyrical qualities and subject matters tend to inspire me the most and the quickest

[87] W. B. Yeats' wife, Georgie Hyde-Lees, wrote words on paper while she was in a deep sleep or trance. This action of hers called automatic writing fascinated Yeats for many years. I recall that it was one of the few things about her that got his attention.

[88] From Yeats' *The Second Coming*

[89] Isaiah 46:10

[90] This highly symbolic warning from Cupid to his wife Psyche is an adaptation of a scene in Lucius "Africanus" Apuleius's *The Golden Asse*. At the point of this comment in the story, Psyche does not know who her husband is. He only comes at night in absolute darkness and refuses to reveal his identity. Later, Psyche listens to her sisters and plots to discover her husband's identity. When oil falls on him from her lamp as she watches him sleep, he awakes and flees, leaving Psyche to be punished for this and other indiscretions by Cupid's mother Venus. Only after Psyche completes several seemingly impossible tasks assigned by Venus and after Cupid begs Jupiter to override his mother's wrath with his bride are the unlikely couple reunited.

[91] Though the poem needs no explanation, I think it is important to note that this is a rehash of a sweet, sentimental poem that, quite frankly, was not much good. Since this poem is to fit in *Atheists and Empty Spaces*, I chose to give it dark undertones as if the words were coming from a narcissist.

[92] This line is the first line of John Donne's *The Curse*. The rhyme scheme and the form also follow Donne's model more or less. However, I do abandon the rhythm of his shorter lines for continuous iambic pentameter.

[93] A Hebrew man consecrated to God who must not drink any alcoholic beverages, cut his hair, or have physical contact with a corpse. The Biblical hero Samson from the book of Judges is the nazirite called to mind here.

[94] *Tropes*, here a pun for *ropes*, is a figure of speech or the use of figurative language. Portraying Delilah as a loving wife would, indeed, be a new and unused trope, at least to my knowledge.

[95] Samson told Delilah that if he were bound with new and unused *ropes* he would lose his strength. It turned out to be a lie.

[96] After Samson was captured by the Philistines, his eyes were gouged out.

[97] Delilah is not mentioned again in Samson's story after she has shorn Samson's hair and cries out that the Philistines are there to get him. Ironically, *the Lord* departs from Samson in the same verse.

[98] I must note that *life* here is used as a synonym for both *reality* and *nature*.

[99] This poem is a conversation that does NOT take place in Genesis 1:6 when Adam is offered the fruit of the tree of the knowledge of good and evil and takes it. People often believe that a conversation takes place here between Adam and Eve, but there is no indication of a conversation in the Bible.

[100] Lingua is Latin for tongue and is still widely used in medical and scientific terminology. Lingua also refers to something that resembles a common language.

[101] Adam literally means "red earth," so his roots are in the ground.

[102] Bringers of dreams refers to angel mostly. Gabriel is, of course, the most famous of these Bringers from the Gospel of Luke. Another Bringer who is often a liar is celebrated by the character Mercutio in *Romeo and Juliet.* She is the famous fairy Queen Mab.

[103] The "forbidden fruit" was from the Tree of Knowledge of Good and Evil.

[104] The Nephilim or sons of gods found in Genesis 6:1-2.

[105] Lilith is a well-represented figure in non-Biblical Jewish traditions. She is the first wife of Adam and, sometimes, the first wife of Satan. She is a demon who steals men's sperm to fertilize other demons, and she also steals babies. I do not know of any tradition that portrays her as a snake. I am original in that as far as I know.

[106] To purl is to jabber, chatter, or generally talk nonsense.

[107] Transpire is used here to mean secreting water in the form of a vapor usually through a living cell.

[108] In Shakespeare's *The Merchant of Venice, Act 2, Scene 7,* the Prince of Morocco says, "All that glisters is not gold," as he seeks to choose the correct casket or box of treasure to win Portia's hand. Our misspeaking of this phrase has become "All that glitters is not gold." I prefer the word "glisters" myself. I cannot say why I wanted to footnote this.

[109] Referring to Matthew 5:45-The sun shines on the wicked and the good; the rain falls on the just and the unjust.

[110] The rainbow, the symbol denoted in the Bible as God's promise not to destroy all of life on Earth with a flood ever again in Genesis 9:12-17, is implied here as a reminder also to the rain.

[111] This poem has some rather interesting origins. With no poetic inspiration for a few weeks, I opened a copy of my *Purple and Blue Collection of Poems* and flipped through it looking for any mention of "empty spaces" or "atheists" to maintain the themes of the current collection. When I finally came to the words "empty spaces" in a poem, I grabbed the copy of *Hamlet* that sits on my writing desk and flipped to a random page. Then, I said, to myself, that I would connect the ideas of my old poem—not one that I particularly like, by the way—and the idea presented on that page in *Hamlet* in some manner that creates a coherent poem of ideas. I think it worked out pretty well as sign o' the times.

[112] Here, I mean the worship of physical, material objects.

[113] In Victor Hugo's *Et Nox Facta Est*, Satan ran or, actually, flew in circles for ten thousand years trying to escape infinity before he stopped to rest, broken, tired, and panting.

[114] William Blake's narrator in the poem *London* marked in every face he met, "marks of weakness, marks of woe."

[115] A unit for transmitting cultural ideas and practices through writing, speech, bodily gestures, symbols, etc.

[116] In *Hamlet*, Act II, Scene II, Hamlet claims that he could be bound in a nutshell and still be counted the king of infinite spaces if it were not for bad dreams.

[117] In *Hamlet*, Act IV, Scene V, Ophelia, in madness brought on by Hamlet's rejection and accidental murder of her father, distributes flowers to Laertes (her brother), King Claudius, and Queen Gertrude. She calls "rue" the herb of grace or repentance, but "rue" also means regret or sorrow. Laertes says that she makes "hell itself" pretty. The next report of Ophelia is that she has drowned in a pool of water with her "weedy trophies."

[118] Here the idea *admiration* is given substance as the mythological Greek Gorgon Medusa.

[119] French Catholic-priest-turned-atheist-philosopher Jean Meslier called *admiration* the daughter of ignorance in the 18th century. I am not inventing that idea.

[120] The word *delusions* works very well here because a delusion causes someone to believe in an idea or ideal that does not compare with the physical or factual reality.

[121] In Ovid's version of the Medusa myth, Medusa is given serpents for hair as part of her punishment for allowing Poseidon to rape her in Athena's temple. In other versions, she is the only Gorgon to have been born with snakes for hair.

[122] Admiration, like both wonder and awe, tend to be short-lived and ephemeral. None of them last long, but unlike admiration, wonder and awe do not often end in disappointment in the "worshipped" subject.

[123] One glance upon the face of Medusa turned the viewer to stone. Some of those turned to stone by Medusa's glance were the titan Atlas, the sea monster Cetus who was sent to kill Andromeda (often portrayed as the Kraken), and King Polydectes and the wicked members of his court.

[124] The golden giant Chrysaor, sometimes the brother of Pegasus, and the famed white winged horse Pegasus sprang from the blood of Medusa. In some stories, they sprang straight from her severed neck. Chrysaor is a symbol of wealth, and Pegasus is a symbol of poetry.

[125] Admirers often turn worshippers when the admired shows approval.

[126] Perseus was sent to get the head of Medusa when he showed up at a marriage banquet without a gift of a horse for King Polydectes. Having not brought a gift, Perseus agreed to procure any gift the King named. Polydectes, hoping to kill Perseus so that he might marry his mother, sent him on a death errand to retrieve Medusa's head. Therefore, Medusa's head was a party favor or a gift at a party.

[127] No one could fathom Medusa's emotional state from her face because all who saw it were turned to stone. A reproduction of her face could be found as a symbol on Athena's shield. The Greek word *Medusa* actually translates as "to guard or protect."

[128] The capitalization of the pronoun means that it refers to God or Yahweh.

[129] These "cryptic pages" are, of course, the pages of the Bible.

[130] The irony is that humans believe that they could experience eternity as something that is comparable to the human understanding of time, which is probably not ironic but absurd.

[131] To immure can mean to entomb within a wall, which is part of the myth built around the Christ-figure. Jesus was a human and, thus, was a god with whom priests, the Pharisees and Sadducees, bargained or argued. I think that religious leaders still use these ancient ideas of demigods and demi-men to bargain over what the ideas of Christianity are and should be though we no longer create Suffering Messiah figures for contemporary consumption. The death of Superman in DC Comics a few years ago might have been the closest American society has come to producing a popular Suffering Messiah figure in quite some time.

[132] The idea of a mortal god is what some would call a paradox.

[133] I am emphasizing here the idea that, if there were a singular moment of creation by a god, why that god could not have intended that evolution occur to produce all things rather than producing all things at once. Who would know the intent of a god with this kind of power?

[134] This stanza points out several traits of religious zealots. They all question the faith of those who do not agree with them. They all think that they live in unique and wicked times. They all believe that they are the ones intended to announce, judge, pronounce, and condemn the wickedness of their times. I do not include this, but they all tend to think that they are living in the end times.

[135] According to many experts in Hebrew, nearly 75% of the Christian-called Old Testament is written in poetry, which is clearly seen in Proverbs, Song of Solomon, and Psalms but perhaps less clearly seen in the books of prophecy such as Isaiah and Jeremiah. Therefore, to understand most of what is going on in the Tanakh or Hebrew Bible, followers would need to be students and even scholars of poetry not only in the language which they speak but students of Hebrew poetry of ancient times. Good luck with that.

[136] Neap tides occur during the quarter and three quarter moon and have the least difference between high and low tides. Tides are caused by the gravitational pull of the moon.

[137] *Blithe* can mean cheerful and happy, but it also means carefree and indifferent.

[138] Nietzsche, with whom I do not often agree, believes that the "will to power" is an evolutionary guide to dominate everything within a particular ecosystem or environment. He believed that even plants have this will to power, and it is what causes certain plants and animals to succeed and others to fail. I am saying, in my short poem, that once the human dominates the ecosystem or environment, it wants all the other natural occurrences, the "natural will to power," to stop doing what it does.

[139] Science is a myth as it provides an explanation for why things are the way they are. It is also a myth in that many of the current scientific views will likely be changed to more accurate descriptions as technology and the scientific method improves. Whether science remains mythical or not, the methods by which science is conducted try to maintain objectivity. Thus, a personal, loving bond with nature can not represent a scientific view of the world.

[140] Principles tend to be abstract ideas that form a foundation for beliefs or behavior as established by reason or logic not through emotional, physical, or biological connections.

[141] To stick with the theme of this poem, I will not footnote the people or the terms in this poem. Go look up the authors and the words!

[142] This poem centers around the unique, weird, and taboo ideas of love associated with the Greek myths of King Minos of Crete

[143] Icarus, with a set of wings designed by his father Daedalus, flew too close to the sun, melted the wax holding his wings together, and plunged to his death.

[144] Daedalus built the labyrinth for King Minos in which was imprisoned the Minotaur, who was the son of Minos' wife Pasiphae and the Cretan bull.

[145] Theseus killed the Minotaur with the help of Minos' daughter Ariadne, who provided him with a string to lead him back out of the labyrinth. According to some legends, Theseus abandoned Ariadne on the island of Naxos when he tired of her charms.

[146] The Titan Prometheus denied the gods and gave humans the gift of fire.

[147] This was originally a much shorter poem that dealt with a sexual awakening rather than an artistic awakening. Maybe the sexual part is still there, but I do not know if it is still the most important theme in the poem.

[148] In the 1970's and '80's, painters in the Stone County area of Arkansas started using the round, sawmill blades that were three or four feet or bigger as canvasses and were willing to pay as much as $500 for one. This sent a lot of people out looking around in the woods for these old blades because they were generally rolled off behind a sawmill somewhere as they had no other use. I was one of those runners, but I never got lucky and found one.

[149] This character was originally pretty Satanic.

[150] Mary's response to Gabriel in Luke 1:38

[151] This is a variation of an expression in Coleridge's *Biographia Literia*. I have not located the exact quote.

[152] "Conception" holds the dual meanings of becoming pregnant and forming ideas and thoughts.

[153] This poem is a tribute to and inspired by Tennyson's *Ulysses*. Here I create another "end" for the great Greek warrior, hero, and trickster Odysseus

[154] "It" is the future or the hearer of his tale in the future.

[155] George Gordon (Lord) Byron and Leonard Cohen. The title of the poem is the same as the title of Byron's poem upon which this is modelled.

[156] Pope says:

"Know, then, thyself, presume not God to scan; The proper study of mankind is man."

[157] The "perfect chord" and most of this line come from Cohen's *Hallelujah*.

[158] From Percy Shelley's *Queen Mab: A Philosophical Poem*, Part 7, lines 13 and 14.

[159] A traditional Southern staple named due to their size, my Grandma Thomas made these nearly every day of her life when she was able.

[160] Sudden Infant Death syndrome, as yet unnamed and unknown when the character is young

[161] Though this poem is about many men that I have known, it was my father who suffered from polio, he did live with his Grandpa and Grandma (Ma and Pa), and he did drag himself around on the porch. He also went to work in the log woods at around thirteen but not because his mother was sick. Other parts of this story do not come from my dad's life story.

[162] Many Christians still associate disease and disaster with God's punishment for sin.

[163] A small still of the type most people have seen in movies or on TV with a round pot boiler, a cap, and copper tubing condenser.

[164] Made of sheets of copper or galvanized steel nailed together, these boilers could hold hundreds of gallons of mash

[165] Revenuers are the federal agents associated with the Internal Revenue Service, who sought to collect taxes on the alcohol made. They are generally seen as pretty "bad"

people by bootleggers. The "wars" between bootleggers and revenuers are the subject of many a movie and song.

[166] As a boy, it seemed to me that nearly every woman in Stone County worked at the Blanchard Shirt Factory. As I got older, I realized that was not quite true.

[167] A song of spiritual warfare from around the turn of the 20th century. Personally, I find it hypocritical, unrealistic, and confrontational. The first line is the complete title.

"Let's take the land! The land that God has given us;
In all our living, Christ can be so much:
To take this land, we have th' equipment that we need—
The blood, the Word, the Spirit, and the church.

     Sisters:
Let's take the land! O Christian brothers,
The land that God has given us.
Be strong and take it, for we can make it
And gain this land so glorious!
Brothers:
Let's take the land! O Christian sisters,
And to these things give earnest heed.
The Lord implores us; He's gone before us
And given everything we need!

We have the blood! Christ is our spotless offering,
Who gave Himself, our God to satisfy;
And so we come with boldness to the throne of grace,
And all day long, the precious blood apply.

We have the Word! The written Word's our daily food;

We mix this Word with faith and say "Amen!"
Then thro' the day, the spoken Word will speak to us
And regulate our living from within.

The Spirit's ours! The Spirit of reality,
He's independent of the way we feel;
He dwells in us, and teaches us to dwell in Him,
And guides us into everything that's real.

We have the church! All saints are needed to possess
The fullness of this vast reality;
Together we will gain this all-inclusive Christ,
And He to us our everything will be."

[168] Believe it or not, this image of Johnny is an exact image of someone that I knew whose name cannot be mentioned because he may still be up to the same thing.

[169] One of my sons' school friends was stabbed to death during a suspected deal gone bad in around 2008 or so.

[170] I realize that both slang words "script" for "prescription" and "opies" for "opiods" would not have been used in the time nor the geographical area presented in this poem, but it helped me with the rhyme and rhythm.

[171] A man that I know refused to put a headstone on his wife's grave because she had committed suicide. After he died, a church provided her with a stone marker. I do not know who provided his.

[172] Short for moonshine, of course

[173] I actually spent many years hauling stone to make extra money with my good friend Charles "Chuck" Hastings, but

we never used an Army surplus truck. Other field stone haulers often used old Army trucks.

[174] These stories told to me by Tollie Leonard were based in the Pacific theater during World War II. To the best of my recollection, Tollie was in an engineering division of the Army though I honestly am not sure which branch of the Armed Forces he served in.

[175] The story about Laocoön (pronounced *lay-ah-ka-wahn*) that I have known best is from Book II of Virgil's *The Aeneid*. Laocoön pleads with King Priam and the leaders of the Trojans to destroy the wooden horse left for them by the Greeks as it sits on the beach where the Greek ships had been. When they will not listen, he throws a spear at the horse, and it plunges deeply into the hollow horse with a sound that should have confirmed that the gift was a ruse. However, a captured Greek named Sinon tells a tale of Odysseus' treachery against him and how he seeks to only do the Greeks harm, so he tells them that the wooden horse is harmless, and he is believed by the Trojans. Later, as Laocoön prepares a sacrifice to Poseidon, two sea serpents come and kill Laocoön and his two boys. The serpents then go and lie at the feet of the statue of Athena in her temple. This confirms to the Trojans that Laocoön's "false" claims were an affront to the gods of Olympus, and they pull the wooden horse into Troy, which leads to their utter destruction.

[176] Laocoön was sacrificing a bull or steer to the gods when the serpents arrived.

[177] Another name for the Greeks but broadly of or relating to Greece

[178] The wooden horse was constructed by Odysseus on advice from Athena. He and his men hid within it. Agamemnon's fleet was not defeated. It was merely out of sight in a nearby bay waiting for the signal from Odysseus and his men that they had opened the gates of Troy to let the Greek armies in.

[179] This poem seems an imitation of John Keats' *Ode to a Nightingale*. However, in reality, it is a re-make of my poem *Suicide Note*, written in 1998, which is a very poor imitation of Keats' poem. It can be found on page 341 in *The Purple and Blue Collection of Poems: Volumes I and II*, which has become my primary source of inspiration because of its good ideas but lazy and ignorant craftsmanship.

[180] The question that runs throughout this poem is this: Is the narrator a bird or is it a poet or bard? The answer is this: both or one or the other, but it is not neither. It is a bird or a bard or both, but when and where? That depends upon what part is being read. As I wrote this, I thought that it was always both, but as I read it, I think I accidentally made it one or the other at different places.

[181] Here, in mock novelty, I move the short line to the seventh rather than the sixth as in Keats' poem.

[182] Keats' exact words in *Ode to a Nightingale*. I do not believe there are any more word combinations that are exactly the same.

[183] I amused myself with this line considering the current state of American politics and its justice system and the more contemporary term for the Latin *quid pro quo*.

[184] The purple thistle has long fascinated me. It is a beautiful member of the sunflower family with its purple or pink flowers and fine hair-like structures on its leaves and stems that seem to glow in the dim light of the moon or at dawn or evening. However, my experience with it as a farmer is that it is a prolific, hardy, and persistent weed that no grazing animal will eat. It quickly infests hay fields and is a very thorny and painful plant to handle. It also resists herbicides and spreads millions of seeds even while dying. It is a booger to get it out of fields.

[185] I think this is the fifth revision of this poem, but I will admit that it could be the fourth or the seventh. However, I do know that I always go to the version of the poem on page 344 of *The Purple and Blue Collection of Poems: Volumes I and II* whenever I start to revise. It was not a bad poem for its part in my juvenilia.

[186] As I noted earlier, because of the fine white hairs (I do not know what else to call them.) on the leaves of the purple thistle, they often appear to glow in dim light.

[187] Both Black-eyed Susan and Queen Anne's Lace are common weedy flowers found in fields in Arkansas. Black-eyed Susan is a coneflower. Queen Anne's Lace, the wild carrot, is also known as Bishop's Lace or Bird's Nest.

[188] The purple thistle symbolically represents the mocking of Jesus in a couple of ways. The Roman soldiers dressed him in a purple robe and placed a crown of thorns on his

head and "worshipped" him as their king. Actually, the purple thistle is covered in thorns and has purple on its head. That would be exactly the opposite, I suppose.

[189] Of course, a plant, even if it could think, would not suffer as it has no nerve network, but, like Hamlet, "Nay, not seems but is…" simply exists. It does not interpret its existence. It is.

[190] The sign translated here is that the purple thistle is probably a "lunatic" or literally a lover of the moon.

[191] When Kellie first read this poem, she noted that in this line, the poem shifts from a mystical, majestic, and mythical style of language to a practical, simple, and rustic style. I cannot lie and say that I intended that to happen, but it seems that she is right.

[192] This word, pronounced exactly like "cherry," means hesitant and vigilant about dangers and risks. The moon in the rest of the poem was soothing, singing, and loving or loved.

[193] I revised this poem after reading some appalling verse in an addition of contemporary "poetry" in a publisher's catalog. The verse, as with most contemporary "poetry," was basically prose that was very conversational language arranged in verse-like lines. There was no attempt to establish or maintain rhythm or meter, and I could not see that the "poets" made any attempt to elevate their meaning through word choice. I do not believe that all poems have to rhyme nor that they have to be metrical and rhythmic. However, I do believe that, in some sense, all that is POETRY must display the poet's awareness of how the

sound echoes the sense and how word choice is used to present what "oft was thought but ne'er so well expressed" (Pope.) Even a novice in poetry can recognize when a poet is careful in his or her word choice and when the sound of a poem read aloud enhances its meaning. People who write verse that does not cause this recognition are not writing bad poetry; they are not writing poetry. They are doing something else. I do not know what. I hope that you recognize that I am always careful with the sound of my poems and the word choice. Whether the poems are good or not, well…I suppose I have to defer to my readers.

[194] This poem is inspired by and takes many of its themes from Matthew Arnold's *The Buried Life*.

[195] Hopefully, some readers will get my pun that "arrears" sounds like "our ears." It may be a Southern thing.

[196] An allusion to Shakespeare's lines spoken by Juliet: "A rose by any other name would smell as sweet."

[197] The model of the rolling stone is that it gathers no moss. People who always move show very little responsibility or care for others.

[198] Another dream poem inspired by the works of John Keats. The original title is *A Quiet Mourning*, but revisions of the poem changed the theme.

[199] This poem contains so many references to classic rock music that I could never remember all of them. I will try to note what I can. The title was originally *An Old Fashioned Love Song* like the song by the band Three Dog Night.

[200] Often called the greatest of King Arthur's knights, he was also known as the lover of the King's wife Guinevere.

[201] Lady Elaine of Astolat or Shallot feel deeply in love with Lancelot and died of grief when he did not return to her.

[202] Wife of King Arthur but lover of Lancelot

[203] Sandro Botticelli's painting *The Birth of Venus* from the 1480's

[204] According to a study that I read once, watermelon and licorice were the two odors that women found the most sensual. Watermelon does not work in the metrical scheme of the poem, so I chose lime, which was a little further down on the "sensual smell" list.

[205] Louisiana, the home of the Louisiana State University Tigers

[206] The book is by S. E. Hinton and is set in Oklahoma City in the 1960's. The movie is by Francis Ford Coppola

[207] These lines mimic *Stopping by Woods on a Snowy Evening*

[208] Seize the day!

[209] The following lines are a tribute to the kiss of Don Juan and Haidee in Canto II of Byron's *Don Juan*.

[210] This poem is inspired by the lines of Marcellus in Shakespeare's *Hamlet*. I actually cut Marcellus' lines put them in a document by themselves and made the number of my lines match with the number of lines Marcellus spoke. If I missed one or two, it was not an exact science.

[211] *The Purple and Blue Collection of Poems: Volumes I and II (1982-1998)*, Writers Club Press, 2001.

[212] End of page 326

[213] By "chimerical" here, I mean fantasy-like rather than the mythological female creature with a lion's head, a goat's

body, and a serpent's tale—though that image does work with the poem.

[214] The following story is true as best as I remember it. I will admit that I infer that the ladies playing volleyball are wearing a certain name brand, but I was not close enough to see whether they were or not. There was another encounter with the church lady in the blue swimsuit at the creek that I have left out for brevity's sake. She slipped on a large mossy rock, and I helped her up. Also, the girl passed me on the bicycle several more times than I put in the poem though she never did wave at me while riding the bike—as best I remember.

[215] The Blanchard Springs National Forest in northern Stone County, Arkansas is one of the most beautiful areas that I have ever seen. Though I have spent my whole life since a young child visiting the cave, parks, and creeks in the National Forest, it has never lost the sense of awe that it inspires in me. The natural beauty there is breathtaking. I was lucky for it to be within a short drive of my home.

[216] Pronounced "vittles" as Granny Moses would on *The Beverly Hillbillies*.

[217] From Mel Brook's movie *History of the World: Part I*, spoken by the character Torquemada

[218] Although the serpent is described only as "crafty" in *Genesis*, the fruit is described as "pleasing to the eye and tempting to contemplate."

[219] The venerable, supposed author of *The Iliad* and *The Odyssey*. The arming of the warriors is one of the epic conventions.

[220] The jester of Oberon, King of the Fairies. He is also called Robin Goodfellow in English folklore. He is known to be mischievous, lazy, and generally useless except when a laugh is needed. I do not know that he has a brother, but if he did, that is what the other one acted like.

[221] Samuel Taylor Coleridge's poem *Youth and Age* has a narrator who find himself troubled with the reality of growing old and the positive traits that are lost in this inevitability. I maintain this theme in a conversation between younger and older self, but I do not use his form at all. The form is more Keatsian than Coleridgian.

[222] Baudelaire called poetry a priesthood with a membership that was cursed.

[223] A tribute to Tennyson's Ulysses, who will "drink life to the lees."

[224] I cannot possibly relay how tired I am of seeing diary entries presented in uneven lines of broken prose being called "poetry." If the general reading public gets some sort of kick out of reading these diary entries, I cannot pretend to account for its taste, but, please, can we stop referring to whatever it is they are doing as poetry?

[225] I had written this poem down to the line "The simple often lose important parts" many years ago, and I loved the poem to that point, but I had nowhere else to go. I had no story. I have had time to wonder, now: Should I have left it at the word "parts?"

[226] Jim Morrison's poem *The Celebration of the Lizard* contains his famous proclamation "I am the Lizard King/I can do anything." The same poem talks about a game of

forgetting your name. Morrison is said to have claimed that "Morrison" was not his real name and that everyone in his family was dead. None of which, from what I gather, is true.

227 Absent Without Leave

228 Also known as *malebolgia* from Dante's *Inferno*.

229 In Exodus 33:21-22, Moses asked God if he could see him. God told Moses to hide in a cleft in the rock, which God covered with His hand until He had passed. Moses only got to see God's backside.

230 Here, I intend the word to mean evenly balanced.

231 For another comment about pedants and sophists, check out Ursula Le Guin's *The Ones Who Walk Away From Omelas*.

232 In Yeats' *The Second Coming*, he writes that "Things fall apart; the centre cannot hold;/Mere anarchy is loosed upon the world..." These pedants and sophists agree with Yeats that traditional institutions (formal art aesthetics) no longer serve to give art meaning. I disagree—And that is why I write a poem that includes their views.

233 *Lunatic Fringe* by the band Red Rider

234 Friedrich Nietzsche in *Beyond Good and Evil* provided the aphorism, "He who fights with monsters should be careful lest he thereby becomes a monster. And if thou gaze long into an abyss, the abyss will also gaze into thee." This saying fits with my theme although most people believe that he is saying that gaining too much knowledge can take away innocence.

235 Funfair is another word for carnival or sideshow.

236 Reminiscent of Renaissance artist Parmigianino's *Portrait of the Artist in a Convex Mirror*

237 These last two lines sort of reflect Macbeth's "Tomorrow and tomorrow…" speech in *Macbeth Act 5: Scene 5.*

238 I do not know how many different collections of poems I may ever have, but, like Tennyson with *Crossing the Bar*, I think I will insist that all of my collections end with this tribute to Anne Bradstreet's *The Author to Her Book.*